MW00609061

Praise for *Profit Pillars*

"Parker Stevenson demystifies the financial side of running an online business. I appreciate the way he shares his money wisdom with simplicity and practicality. For many of us creatives, money talk can feel daunting—Parker supports us to step into financial ownership and face our financial world while navigating growing our businesses."

—Carrie-Anne Moss, Award-Winning Actress
and Founder, Annapurna Living

"We have been working with Parker and his team at Evolved Finance since 2014. His expertise in dealing with the financial side of online businesses has been a win for us. If you're a digital entrepreneur, you are sure to find a lot of value here."

—Zach Rocklin, CEO, Gabrielle Bernstein, Inc.

"As a medical doctor who helps women with troubles often considered 'taboo' for public discourse, I had no idea, until I read *Profit Pillars*, that people would rather talk about their sex lives than their personal finances. Thank you, Parker, for lifting the veil on this complex topic, in a way that also lifts shame, overwhelm, and confusion for entrepreneurs as we travel the road less taken."

—Aviva Romm, MD, Yale School of Medicine, and
New York Times Bestselling Author, *Hormone Intelligence*

"Success in small business requires solid financial foundations. And yet, so many entrepreneurs fear finance. I get why; it's usually an unnatural skill, and conventional ways of learning finance suck. That fear and avoidance create a big gap in one's potential as a small business owner. *Profit Pillars* fills that gap. It's the book I wish I had 13 years ago when I launched my first start-up company. I'll never build and grow a small business again without referencing *Profit Pillars'* principles and methods. You shouldn't either."

—Matt Gartland, Serial Entrepreneur,
Start-up Advisor, and Angel Investor

"If you're an online business owner wanting a strong financial foundation, you must pick up a copy of *Profit Pillars*. Trust me; no one gets the ins and outs of financial wellness for online businesses like Parker. In *Profit Pillars*, he lays out exactly how to build financial systems that will help you make bank! This book is a must-have for every business owner's bookshelf."

—Lauren Messiah, Coach, Personal Stylist, and
Author, *Style Therapy: 30 Days to Your Signature Style*

"I wish I had this book a decade ago! If I'd known (and implemented) the profitability fundamentals in these pages, I would have saved myself so much time and energy. But I'm so grateful to know and use them now to support my profitable online business. I'll be recommending this book to everyone in my community who has an online business as a must-read!"

—Kate Northrup, Author, *Do Less*

"*Profit Pillars* unveils the essential road map to financial success in the digital age. Delving deep into the untold truths about money, Stevenson guides readers through a transformative journey of self-discovery and financial empowerment. From unraveling personal money narratives to mastering the intricacies of online entrepreneurship, each chapter unveils indispensable insights and actionable strategies. Readers of this book are sure to discover the foundational principles of financial stability, as Stevenson reveals the three critical financial functions essential for online business success. At the heart of the book lie the four Profit Pillars, illuminating the path to sustainable profitability and business growth. With expert guidance on optimizing profitability and navigating the intricacies of self-compensation, *Profit Pillars* is the ultimate guidebook for modern entrepreneurs seeking to build a solid financial future."

—Clint Salter, 5x Exit Entrepreneur

" This book will change the way online business owners think about their finances—both personally and professionally. *Profit Pillars* will empower digital entrepreneurs with the knowledge they need to take control of their finances. Readers of this book will discover that there is no such thing as being 'bad with numbers.' Financial literacy is a learnable skill, and Parker teaches it better than anyone in the online business space."

—David Berry, Founder, RULE13 Learning, and
Author, *More Human Than Otherwise*

"Even though I run a successful business, I'm not naturally a 'numbers person' and always felt that managing my business finances was stressful and confusing. It didn't help that there are so few reliable financial resources for online business owners specifically. No one is better positioned to teach online business owners how to take control of their finances than Parker Stevenson. *Profit Pillars* clearly and easily lays out the specific systems online business owners can use to effectively manage their finances for optimal profitability. This is the book I wish I'd had as a new business owner, and it's one I'll rely on even now that I've been running an online business for years."

—Abbey Ashley, Founder, The Virtual Savvy

"*Profit Pillars* is the book I wish I had when I first started my own financial therapy practice 25 years ago. I had just finished my Masters degree in Psychology and was all too aware that we did not receive any business financial training. Parker Stevenson's new book empowers online business owners to learn about bookkeeping, cash flow, and how to achieve profitability—basically all the financial essentials of running a successful business. He also humanizes finances in a way that helps folks overcome psychological blocks that could prevent them from making healthy financial business decisions. As a financial therapist, I believe *Profit Pillars* should be part of every online business owner's toolkit for financial wellness."

—Bari Tessler Linden, Financial Therapist and
Author, The Art of Money books

" Most online business owners are in the dark on their finances, and as a result, never quite make the money they should be making from their business. The good news is, you're likely closer than you think to a lot more wealth. Parker addresses that head-on in this powerful yet easy-to-read book. The four Profit Pillars will change the game for you and your business. So, stop what you're doing, read *Profit Pillars*, and start gaining the financial success you know is possible."

—Austin Netzley, Founder and CEO, 2X

"Parker Stevenson understands the nuances of entrepreneurial finance and how it applies to online businesses more than anyone. His book, *Profit Pillars*, breaks it down in ways that only true experts mentoring thousands of entrepreneurs can translate in ways that make sense. If you want to be profitable, Stevenson can show you how."

—Amanda Steinberg, Founder, DailyWorth, and Author, *Worth It*

"After building two million-dollar businesses, I landed myself in bankruptcy because I had to learn what Parker Stevenson shares with you in *Profit Pillars* the hard way. The good news for me is that the learnings I gained led to me building an 8-figure online enterprise. The good news for you is that you don't have to go bankrupt to get these lessons. You can just read Parker's book. If you find yourself hiding from the numbers of your life and business, overwhelmed by the complexities of finance, and unable to read a spreadsheet, *Profit Pillars* breaks down the barriers, making financial literacy in business accessible and— believe it or not—enjoyable! And, it could even keep you from going bankrupt. Read on, my friends!"

—Ali Katz, CEO and Founder, Eyes Wide Open Collective

"*Profit Pillars* is the financial empowerment resource every online business owner needs for running a successful, profitable online business. As someone who works with female leaders, I know that financial overwhelm is common and most don't know where to turn for support. Few people get an education on how making and managing money actually works, but Parker teaches specific systems that are easy for anyone to understand and apply to their online business. This is a powerful book for helping online business owners take control of their finances."

—Julie Santiago, Founder and CEO, We Are The Women

PROFIT PILLARS

A Proven System to Maximize the Bottom Line in Your Online Business

PARKER CHARLES STEVENSON

Matt Holt Books
An Imprint of BenBella Books, Inc.
Dallas, TX

This book is designed to provide accurate and authoritative information about entrepreneurship. Neither the author nor the publisher is engaged in rendering legal, accounting, or other professional services by publishing this book. If any such assistance is required, the services of qualified professionals should be sought. The author and publisher will not be responsible for any liability, loss, or risk incurred as a result of the use and application of any information contained in this book.

Profit Pillars copyright © 2024 by Whitaker Admin, Inc., DBA Evolved Finance

All rights reserved. No part of this book may be used or reproduced in any manner whatsoever without written permission of the publisher, except in the case of brief quotations embodied in critical articles or reviews.

Matt Holt is an imprint of BenBella Books, Inc.
10440 N. Central Expressway
Suite 800
Dallas, TX 75231
benbellabooks.com
Send feedback to feedback@benbellabooks.com

BenBella and *Matt Holt* are federally registered trademarks.

Printed in the United States of America
10 9 8 7 6 5 4 3 2 1

Library of Congress Control Number: 2024022702
ISBN 9781637745670 (hardcover)
ISBN 9781637745687 (electronic)

Editing by Katie Dickman
Copyediting by Michael Fedison
Proofreading by Denise Pangia and Jenny Bridges
Indexing by Debra Bowman
Text design and composition by PerfecType, Nashville, TN
Cover design by Brigid Pearson
Cover image © Shutterstock / bsd studio
Printed by Lake Book Manufacturing

Special discounts for bulk sales are available. Please contact bulkorders@benbellabooks.com.

I dedicate this book to:
Corey Whitaker, you are not just my business partner. You are my family.
The Evolved Finance team, for serving our clients with such
care. I appreciate all of you more than you will ever know.
The Evolved Finance clients—without your trust and
belief, this book would not have been written.

CONTENTS

Release of Liability xi

Who Should Read This Book? xiii

Introduction 1

PART 1: FINANCIAL MINDSET 9

Chapter 1: What They Do Not Teach You About Money
in School 11

Chapter 2: What Is Your Money Story? 23

Chapter 3: The Two Financial Games of Online
Entrepreneurship 37

**PART 2: BUILDING YOUR FINANCIAL
FOUNDATION** 53

Chapter 4: The Hidden Impact of Your Personal Finances 55

Chapter 5: The Three Financial Functions of an Online Business... 77

Chapter 6: Creating a Clean Financial Foundation 109

PART 3: THE FOUR PROFIT PILLARS 131

Chapter 7: The Goal of the Profit Pillars System . . .
Generate a Profit! 133

Chapter 8: The Four Profit Pillars of Your Online Business 147

Chapter 9: Using Your Profit Pillars to Fix Your Profitability. 181

Chapter 10: How to Pay Yourself Without Breaking
Your Business. 209

Your Support System 225

Acknowledgments 231

Index 233

RELEASE OF LIABILITY

Hey there! Parker here to share an important reminder with you. I am not your accountant. I am also not your tax attorney. *Profit Pillars* is not meant to be a replacement for an accountant or a tax attorney. This book is for educational purposes only. Neither myself, nor my company, Evolved Finance, is responsible or liable for any legal or tax issues that you might find yourself in after reading this book. As I state many times throughout the coming chapters, please consult with an accountant or tax attorney in your country to ensure any changes you make to your financial systems and processes comply with your local tax and business laws.

WHO SHOULD READ THIS BOOK?

Before we get started, I think it is important that we get on the same page about what defines the type of online business that this book will be able to help. **If you sell digital products and/or services online, have fewer than 50 employees on your team, and generate less than $25 million a year in revenue**, then you are in the right place. That said, I believe any business owner will benefit from reading the first six chapters of this book. Chapters seven and beyond will be much more tailored to the unique financial needs of online businesses.

The most common types of online businesses that the Profit Pillars system is able to help are:

- **Online educators** selling courses and membership sites.
- **Coaches and consultants** selling individual and group packages.
- **Content creators, influencers, podcasters, and bloggers** making money from sponsorship income and ad revenue.
- **Authors and speakers** making money from book advances, book royalties, and speaking fees.

- **Service providers, freelancers, and agency owners** selling custom or productized service packages that can be fulfilled fully or partially online.
- **Self-funded SaaS companies** selling perpetual or subscription licenses to their software.

Whether you work full-time or part-time in your online business does not matter. Nor does it matter if you are the sole owner of your business or have a business partner. If you meet the criteria above, then this book will teach you everything you need to know about managing the financial side of your business like a boss.

If your business focuses solely on selling physical products (e-commerce), building physical products (manufacturing and crafts), is a local business (restaurant, plumber, boutique retail store, etc.), or is a tech start-up focused on raising capital from investors, then this book will not be tailored to the needs of your business.

Are we on the same page now? Great! Now come meet me in the introduction.

INTRODUCTION

I am a hypocrite.

I rarely read the introductions to books, yet I am asking you to take a moment and read this one because I want you to go into this book with the right frame of mind. As you will quickly learn in chapter one, money can be a stressful (if not terrifying) subject for many online entrepreneurs, so I want to begin our journey together by doing three things:

1. Boost your confidence that you are 100% capable of understanding and executing all of the business/financial concepts discussed in this book.
2. Build some trust that I actually know what the hell I am talking about so you can move forward into the subsequent chapters without hesitation or skepticism.
3. Gain clarity about how you will benefit from reading this book.

First things first. Most online entrepreneurs I talk to think they are bad at the financial side of their businesses. Even the ones who are former accountants or have financial experience from their time in the corporate world still tell me they are confused and/or intimidated about how to keep track of and analyze the flow of money in and out of their businesses. This confusion translates into stress and uncertainty.

1

How can you feel confident about the decisions you make for your business if you don't know how profitable it is, are unclear about how profitable it should be, and have no clue how to start down a path of finding that clarity? Many businesses have failed or squandered their potential because the owner(s) bought into the story that they are bad with numbers and subsequently ignored their numbers altogether or abdicated their financial responsibility to somebody else. Neither option is a good one. Every decision you make in your business has a financial impact. The sooner you understand and accept this, the sooner you will realize how harmful it is to believe you are bad with numbers and finance.

I actually do not believe any online business owner is "bad" at finance. How can you be bad at doing something that nobody has taught you how to do? It is like my two-year-old telling me that they do not like roasted carrots even though they have never even tried them.

When you started your business, how good were you at making sales calls? How good were you at copywriting? Webinars? Hiring? Leadership? I'm willing to bet you did not possess every business skill you currently have today. You probably leaned into what you were good at, but you also learned and developed new business skills. This is what entrepreneurship is all about: learning, adapting, and growing.

So let me say this one more time: You are not bad at finance. You just have not gained the knowledge you need yet to understand how it works for *your* type of business.

Now I am not saying you need to love finance or that you should be spending all your time focusing on numbers instead of the other aspects of your business. I am saying that most online entrepreneurs stick their heads in the sand, completely ignore their businesses's financial sides, and then tell the world they are bad with money.

Luckily, you do not have to be born a math genius or money guru to learn how to build a more financially sound online business. You just have to learn a few basic skills and concepts that you will then be able to leverage for the rest of your entrepreneurial career.

But here lies the problem. Where the hell are you supposed to find a financial expert with years of experience in the online business space who can teach you exactly what you need to know about how money works for an online business?

You can find them right here! Hello!

I've taught thousands of online business owners like you how to build simple and sustainable financial systems that allow them to make more profitable decisions in their businesses. I've been doing this work since 2014 through my accounting and business advising firm, Evolved Finance. The firm was founded by my business partner, Corey Whitaker, in 2010. There is literally nobody else in the world with more financial expertise regarding online businesses than me, Corey, and our amazing team of financial professionals at Evolved Finance.

Just to be clear, most bookkeeping and accounting firms do not coach or educate their clients about their numbers, but in our experience, helping our clients understand what their numbers mean is just as important as ensuring their bookkeeping is done accurately and their tax returns are filed on time.

This is why I created the Profit Pillars systems with my business partner. After years of helping our clients dive into their numbers, I knew there was an easier way to help online business owners understand how money moves through their businesses.

Understanding this movement (also known as cash flow) is one of the most fundamental concepts you can learn as an online business owner. Once you understand how this side of your business works, and you have the systems in place to make sure you and your team can track your finances more clearly, you will see your business become:

1. More profitable
2. Less stressful to manage
3. More stable and predictable
4. A tool to create true personal wealth

The Profit Pillars system allows you to do this without the need to acquire an MBA or hire a CFO. You just need someone to teach you how to build better financial systems in your online business and give you some basic financial metrics you can use to monitor the health of your business.

Believe it or not, you do not even need to be a "numbers person"; most of our clients do not consider themselves to be numbers people. They think of themselves as digital marketers, creatives, and visionaries. Just like they learned how to use email marketing software, host webinars, write sales copy, and leverage social media platforms to find their customers, they also learned how to uplevel their financial literacy.

Just like many of you reading this book, I also believed myself to not be a numbers person. I got a degree in marketing, not in finance or accounting. I got a C in both of my entry-level accounting classes in college. I barely understood how Microsoft Excel worked when I graduated from college in 2004. I could not have imagined an industry I was less interested in than finance and accounting. My goal as a 21-year-old fresh out of undergrad school was to tour the world with my rock band playing sold-out shows (that is a whole other story for another time). As a songwriter and musician, I viewed myself only as a creative and a visionary for many years. Part of that story was rooted in memories of my dad helping me with my elementary school math homework as a kid and breaking into tears of frustration because I struggled with the concepts my dad was trying to teach (thank you for patiently sitting by my side while I had a pity party for myself, Dad!). I let those tear-filled experiences trying to learn fractions and long division shape my self-image until my late twenties when I finally started to appreciate the power of some simple business math and a spreadsheet.

And now?

I've learned to love analyzing the numbers in our clients' businesses and my own business (big emphasis on the word *learned*). While I am not a spreadsheet guru, I am completely comfortable crunching some numbers in a spreadsheet to build a quick forecast or a budget. While I am not an accountant, I understand everything a small business owner needs to know about taxes, including when to bring in the support of a qualified accountant. While I am not a CFO, I can analyze an online business's profit and loss statement and pinpoint any major financial issues with ease.

I learned my financial skills just like the other entrepreneurial skills I did not possess before diving into the business world. Because I was motivated to be a successful, productive, and valuable member of any team I was on (including my own business), I was open to learning any of the skills necessary to make that happen, and I trusted that if others could learn those skills, I could learn them too.

What I am trying to say is that even though, at one point in my life, my only financial knowledge was how to attach a chain wallet to my Dickies pants ('90s punk rock style, anyone?) and my greatest financial accomplishment was winning $5,000 at a battle of the bands concert, I was still able to learn how the financial side of a business works. If someone like me, who had no interest or natural proclivity toward numbers can accomplish this, then I have full confidence you can do it too. Even better, you do not need to know as much about finance as I do. You just have to know enough to build some simple financial systems, make profit-based business decisions, and have productive conversations with your finance team—all things you are going to learn in this book!

I cannot emphasize enough how many online business owners I have worked with over the years at Evolved Finance who have similar stories to mine. Before starting their online businesses, our clients have been therapists, lawyers, artists, designers, stay-at-home parents, athletes, actors, musicians, students, and even quilters! Now they are selling courses, membership sites, coaching programs, consulting packages, online services, software, and sponsorship deals, all while being financially responsible business owners!

If you have had frustrating experiences with your finances in the past, this book is your chance to reset the narrative. I do not care if you had an accountant who was rude and condescending, a bookkeeper who never delivered on what they promised, or you currently have thousands of dollars of debt on your business credit cards. Those experiences do not have to shape your financial future. Now is your chance to get the specific, actionable, and easy-to-understand knowledge you need to run a profitable online business. As long as you can do some elementary school–level math and follow instructions, you can have an online business for which you are actually excited to review your numbers.

One last thing before you move on to chapter one. If you review the table of contents, you will notice that I grouped the chapters of *Profit Pillars* into three main parts. Part one consists of the first three chapters, which focus on developing your financial mindset. Part two contains chapters four through six and focuses on helping you to build or clean up the financial foundation of your online business. Part three includes chapters seven through ten, which teach you everything you need to know about the Profit Pillars system. Things like how to implement the Profit Pillars system into your business's finances, how to analyze the financial health of your online business using the Profit Pillars framework, and how to pay yourself as a business owner.

By grouping the chapters into these three main parts, it will make it easier to refer back to the chapters that you might want to dive deeper into as you implement the strategies of this book into your business.

It is also important to understand that while this book is titled *Profit Pillars*, I purposely put the chapters that are more specific to the Profit Pillars framework in the last four chapters of the book. What will become obvious after you finish reading this book is that there is a very linear path toward integrating the Profit Pillars system into your online business. Each chapter will guide you step-by-step toward this ultimate goal. While part three of this book is the payoff, you will have a ton of "aha!" moments reading parts one and two. What I am ultimately asking of you is to trust the process.

I am so proud of you for taking the financial side of your online business seriously, and I am honored you have chosen this book to help you learn more. I can't wait to dive in with you!

To your financial success!

PART 1

Financial Mindset

The following three chapters focus on shifting your money mindset. After talking with so many online entrepreneurs over the years who struggle with their feelings around money, I felt it was important to share my perspective on the more human aspects of making financial decisions as an entrepreneur. While the Profit Pillars system will make it easier for you to separate your emotions from the financial decisions you have to make as a business owner, doing the work to build a healthier outlook on money will only amplify your ability to make calm and grounded decisions with your money as an entrepreneur.

What They Do Not Teach You About Money in School

I know you just started reading this book, but could you tell me what your favorite sex position is, please?

No?

How about you tell me how much money you have in your bank account instead?

We are only three sentences into the first chapter and you likely feel the urge to punch me in the mouth for asking such intimate and personal questions. I do not blame you.

While both questions are wildly inappropriate to ask someone you have just met, surveys done by financial organizations in both the United States and United Kingdom have shown that the majority of respondents would rather talk about their sex lives than their financial lives.

This is a shocking discovery for two reasons.

The first one being that money is a fundamental thread woven through the fabric of our society. Almost everything we do as humans has some sort of financial implication. We spend most of our waking days working to make money so we can afford our existences. It is an unavoidable aspect of living in any modern capitalistic society, so wouldn't we want to talk about money all the time?

The second reason why these survey results are so surprising, especially for Americans, is because of our puritanical roots. Our culture is known for being far more prudish about sex when compared to most European countries, so to discover that over half of Americans would prefer to reveal an intimate detail of their sex lives over producing a tiny nugget of their personal financial situation goes against a major assumption about American culture. It would not have been an unreasonable hypothesis to guess that more than 80% of Americans answering this survey question would rather talk about money given our history with sex in this country, yet over half defaulted to revealing their favorite sex position over sharing their bank account balance.

While I admit that this survey question is hardly the foundation for an in-depth sociological study, it does uncover that, for many people, the shame, anxiety, and frustration they feel about money is far more potent than any feelings they have about revealing what happens between the sheets.

But why?

Aside from the more banal reasons for not talking about money, like "it is impolite" or "it is rude," many sociologists have come to realize that humans living in capitalistic societies equate their incomes to their value as people. In theory, those with higher incomes have skills that are more sought after, which often comes with higher levels of prestige and status, ultimately creating the perception that people with money are more valuable or, simply stated, are better humans. While most people would agree that your net worth does not equate to your quality as a person, it is undeniable that this money psychology, even if it is not at the front of our conscious minds, floats around in the back of our subconscious. If it did not, we would all gladly share our annual salaries and net worth with everyone we know and not lose a wink of sleep over it.

One thing we do know about humans is that we are hierarchical creatures. When we lay our financial cards on the table for all to see, knowing that we subconsciously link our value in society with the numbers in our bank accounts, we open the door for others to assess where we rank in the unofficial financial caste system. I have no doubt that there are those who could care less about what others think of them, especially when it comes to their money, but research has shown most people fall into the psychological trappings of maintaining status in their communities. The success of luxury brands like Mercedes-Benz, Apple, and Gucci are proof of this.

This is not a personal finance book though. We are here to talk about online business finance. Do not worry, my friend, money psychology is doubly "fun" for you as an entrepreneur. Not only do you get to participate in the emotional circus that all people experience with their personal finances, but you also get to deal with the shame, anxiety, and frustration of being responsible for successfully managing the financial health of your online business too. How's that for extra pressure?

Online business owners are already choosing the path less traveled by venturing out to see if their skills, ideas, and vision have value in the marketplace. They are risking to bypass a more conventional career path to instead bet on whether they have a product and/or service that makes consumers want to pull out their wallets. If consumers do not buy in, though, an extra layer of judgment and self-loathing can arise because the market has essentially told them that it does not value what their business is selling.

I think you are getting the idea here. Money is emotional, it is taboo to talk about, and it is deeply connected to our value and self-worth. It is also severely misunderstood by most people. All of that said, if you have ever felt any sort of negative emotions about your personal or business finances, you are not alone. In fact, you would be in the majority. Intuit, the company that owns QuickBooks Online and TurboTax, conducted a study in 2019 that showed 60% of small business owners felt that they did not know enough about finance and accounting. From my experience as a financial professional in the online space, I'd be willing to bet that close to 70–80% of online business owners feel in the dark about their money because so few of them have backgrounds in business before starting their entrepreneurial careers.

Here is where the mind games get kicked up a notch. While money is a massive component of our daily lives, we assume that everyone else understands how it works except for us. That assumption only makes us feel worse because it leads to the belief that our understanding of money, or lack thereof, is completely our fault. That we somehow missed the seminar on "How to make tons of money, never spend money on anything stupid, and feel waves of joy every time you log into your bank account!"

I am here to tell you that if you feel deficient or insecure about money as an entrepreneur in any way, the blame does not just land on you.

· · · · · ·

I am a big believer in personal responsibility, but when it comes to financial literacy in America and most other countries, we put people at a massive disadvantage when it comes to managing their money. As I mentioned before, online entrepreneurs are particularly vulnerable because their financial literacy is lacking both in their personal finance and in their business's finances.

Let's talk about personal finances for a moment.

I cannot speak for other countries, but America does not make financial literacy a priority at any level of education. Money is only one of the most important tools we utilize in our lifetimes, so why would we need to teach kids about it? In case you missed it, that last question was chock-full of sarcasm.

While there are more states forcing public schools to increase the amount of curriculum around personal financial education, if you are reading this book and were born before 2005, these curriculum changes are not benefiting you. A 2021 survey done by EVERFI showed that only 24% of American high school students demonstrated a proficient level of financial literacy. Yikes!

This number becomes less surprising when we gather some basic statistics about how Americans manage their money:[*†‡]

- About 30–35% of Americans are paying off credit card debt.
- Roughly 70% of students who receive a bachelor's degree have student loan debt at the time of graduation.
- One in three students are at risk of defaulting on their student loans.
- Approximately 40% of Americans have less than three months of living expenses in emergency savings, with half of those having no savings at all.

---

* Sommer, Constance. "Average Credit Card Debt in the U.S." Bankrate, February 28, 2024, https://www.bankrate.com/finance/credit-cards/states-with-most-credit-card-debt/#education-level.

† Bareham, Hanneh. "Survey: Student Loans Have Delayed Wealth-building for Gen Z and Millenial Borrowers." Bankrate, December 6, 2023, Bankrate, December 6, 2023, https://www.bankrate.com/loans/student-loans/financial-milestone-survey.

‡ "Understanding College Affordability," n.d., https://collegeaffordability.urban.org/covering-expenses/borrowing/#/.

Not all of these statistics can be blamed on Americans' lack of financial literacy alone, but there is no question that most people feel unprepared to manage their money and make prudent financial decisions once they become adults. Especially when various economic factors like inflation and stagnant wages make it harder for lower- and middle-class earners to get ahead with their money.

As with most things related to education, if a lesson isn't being taught in the classroom, then one can only hope it is being taught at home. Thankfully, some surveys have shown that parents are having those conversations with their kids. A 2021 T. Rowe Price survey showed that 77% of parents said they frequently talked about money. This is encouraging data, but given how unprepared young adults feel when it comes to managing their money, it is yet to be seen if the conversations happening at home about money are actually fruitful.

When you consider that our education system is not making financial literacy a priority, and that most of our parents are not having in-depth conversations with us about how to successfully manage our money, it is amazing anybody has any damn money at all!

Obviously, there are still people out there who have no credit card debt, have their student loans paid off, and are contributing money into their retirement accounts, but if you are one of the millions of people who feel like you have struggled to make good financial decisions, especially in your teens and twenties, you are not alone. More importantly, how could you have been expected to make the best financial decisions possible if nobody told you how to do it?

• • • • • •

At this point, we understand that our education systems and our parents set up so many of us to struggle with our personal finances. So, should it be any surprise that most online entrepreneurs struggle with their business finances as well? When it comes to personal financial literacy, there are thousands of books, YouTube channels, blogs, and websites dedicated to helping you understand how to budget, invest, and even build a side business to generate some extra income. Finding financial advice for your online business is a different story. If you have been in business for a while, then you know that finding tailored financial guidance for your online business is nearly impossible.

But why?

While there are some common financial principles, strategies, and practices across all businesses, every business model also has its own set of unique financial nuances. This makes it nearly impossible to teach finance to entrepreneurs at a broad scale, because what is a prudent financial strategy for a tech start-up might make zero sense for a restaurant. This is why finding solid financial advice for your online business has probably felt like finding a grain of salt in a sandbox.

If you have a business degree, you likely had to take at least one general finance class. I still remember sitting in my college finance class and absolutely hating it. I was a 20-year-old with no corporate experience, no investing experience, and had far more student debt than I had money in my checking account. The concepts my textbook and professor were trying to teach me were beyond anything I could comprehend because I had no context for how a corporation even functioned. I especially had no comprehension of what the hell a finance department did in a massive corporation.

Perhaps people who went to college for finance, accounting, or entrepreneurship got a better download of how small business finance works? While there is no question that many of these people understand high-level financial concepts and strategies that would go over most other business majors' heads, their expertise lies in the realms of personal finance, corporate finance, and start-up finance. At no point do they take a class that explains to them how money works in an online business.

I know this for a fact because I have coached online business owners who were accountants, finance directors, and certified financial planners in their past careers. I have also worked with online entrepreneurs who have MBAs or law degrees, and some who are even medical professionals. Many of our clients at Evolved Finance have spouses and family members who are certified public accountants, serve as CEOs to nine-figure corporations, work in venture capital, and are agents for the IRS. No matter how educated, intelligent, or connected these online business owners are, they still struggle to find a single source of truth about how the financial side of their online business works.

I share all of this because regardless of whether your finances have been a mild annoyance or a source of crippling anxiety, almost every single online business owner I have talked to feels in the dark about their financial operations. Sure, they file their taxes and pay their bills, but they do not feel like they have strong systems and strategies in place to help them balance building their wealth with keeping their business in good financial standing. It is no wonder most entrepreneurs stick their heads in the sand and just pray they have enough money in their bank accounts each month to cover their bills.

· · · · · ·

Here's the good news.

You can 100% become a numbers person in your business. You might not ever be the CFO for a mega corporation or manage your own hedge fund, but you are fully capable of understanding how money moves in and out of your online business as well as learn to make better financial decisions as the CEO of your company. The kinds of decisions that will make you proud of what you see on your profit and loss statement each month (we'll talk more about your P&L later in the book).

How can I feel so confident about this?

Because I've seen online business owners from various backgrounds and from all parts of the world build their confidence around finance and money with a little bit of help from myself and my team at Evolved Finance. While a handful of our clients have had experience in finance and accounting in their past careers, 99% of them have backgrounds in the arts, sales and marketing, technology, customer service, human resources, education, or some other field completely unrelated to business or finance. In fact, some of our most successful clients had no experience with business or finance before starting their companies. They figured it out as they went along, which, if you have not learned yet, is pretty much how entrepreneurship works in a nutshell—fake it until you make it.

I should tell you at this point that Evolved Finance is not a typical accounting firm. While we do offer bookkeeping, tax planning, and tax preparation services to online business owners, we also make financial education a big part of our service. This is why we have been able to watch our clients transform from people who avoid their finances to online CEOs who feel confident talking about the metrics in their businesses.

We go through this extra effort to educate our clients (and those reading this book) for three reasons:

1. Anyone who can learn the skills and tactics necessary to market and operate their online business is 100% capable of understanding their numbers. Most entrepreneurs will gladly learn how to write better copy, build a landing page, edit a video, use email marketing software, or put together a webinar presentation. If you have learned how to do any of these things, it is because you made the commitment to learn about them. Finance is no different.

2. Finance for online businesses is not as complicated as most people think. While finance for manufacturing businesses, restaurants, and tech start-ups can get messy very quickly, online

businesses benefit from having a very straightforward business model, which makes the financial functions much easier to grasp as well as manage.

3. An online business owner does not need to understand how finance works for other business models. They only need to understand how money works in their online business. That is why our team at Evolved Finance has been able to so effectively help our clients uplevel their financial literacy. The financial principles we teach are narrow and specific to online businesses, which makes our knowledge so much easier to teach compared to what a finance major in college must go through.

I can't emphasize the importance of point #3 enough. The only reason this book is possible is because the financial knowledge I share applies to one type of business model. This is why most accountants and bookkeepers struggle to provide solid financial advice for online businesses. They work with so many different types of businesses with such varying financial needs that it is borderline impossible for them to build up specialized financial expertise. They know a little bit about a lot of different business models, which, in our experience, makes their advice far less powerful and transformational for the business owner.

That does not mean you should not have an accountant or bookkeeper, by the way. At no point in this book do we ever recommend that you file your own taxes or do your own bookkeeping. Accountants and bookkeepers play invaluable roles in your online business, especially if you are lucky enough to find professionals that provide a high level of customer service. That said, you cannot rely on them to teach you the baseline financial knowledge you need to keep your business healthy and your bank account full. That is where this book will be a tremendous resource, regardless of where you are in your entrepreneurial journey.

I do not care if you sell courses about how to train dogs, are a freelance web designer for doulas and midwives, or are a Pokémon card influencer. Not only can you learn how to understand your numbers, but you just might learn to love your numbers as well.

· · · · · ·

In late 2020, I got on a prospect call with an acting coach who, for the sake of this story, we will call Derek. Derek had already had success as a working actor in Los Angeles for a number of years, but along the way, he also built a six-figure coaching business where he helps actors build momentum in their entertainment careers.

Like many artists and creatives, Derek did not think he was a numbers person, so much so that when he filled out his prospective client intake form before our discovery call, he wrote in all capital letters, "NUMBERS SCARE ME." To his credit, Derek also said he was willing to learn how to understand his numbers better, but he was very clear that this part of his business was stressful for him.

At the start of our discovery call, Derek said that we needed to keep the conversation high level. If we started to get too granular regarding anything related to accounting or finance, he would get overwhelmed and shut down. I really appreciated how transparent and vulnerable he was about how he felt, but it did not stop me from inevitably getting too granular. Derek threw his hands up and told me to tone it down on the finance talk. We had a good laugh about it, but he was also speaking his truth. It was stressful for him to start diving into financial concepts that were unfamiliar to him. It opened the floodgates for his mind to panic and tell him, *If you do not understand what Parker is talking about right now, what else do you not know about the financial side of your business?*

After that call, Derek still decided to work with our team at Evolved Finance. What happened from there still inspires me to this day. He opened himself up to learning something new about his business that he had told himself for years he was not good at. After all, he was an actor, an artist, and a coach, not a numbers person. What Derek learned about himself, though, was that he was an online business owner, and just like he learned the skills needed to market and sell his courses and coaching programs, he was able to learn the basic financial skills he needed to be a more effective and confident entrepreneur.

The pride I have for Derek's transformation is immense, but not because what he learned about his business was terribly difficult to comprehend. When framed in the right way, the financial concepts that an online business owner needs to understand are relatively straightforward. What I am proud of is Derek's willingness to push through discomfort. He was able to confront a part of his business that made him feel uncomfortable and anxious, yet he still pushed through that discomfort so he could build the entrepreneurial skills he needed to be successful.

What I hope for you reading this book is that you can find the same bravery and determination in yourself that Derek did, so you can also discover that financial literacy is as learnable as any other skill you have developed since you started your online business. You do not have to be naturally gifted with numbers or have a master's degree in finance. All you need is a desire to learn. If you have that, you might just realize that you are more of a "numbers person" than you thought.

2

What Is Your Money Story?

We all have a money story. Most of us just do not know it yet.

Your money story is a combination of factors that shapes the way you think about, manage, and respond emotionally to money. A lot of business coaches would call this a money mindset, but a poor money mindset is often the result of a problematic money story. Your story shapes and influences your money mindset, which is why I believe it is so important to examine and reflect on your story.

By the end of this chapter, you are going to be much more aware of your own money story. My hope is that by bringing awareness to it, you can stop your money story from negatively affecting the way you manage the money in your business. You are also going to learn a mindset trick I have used with my clients that helps them think about the money in their business in a healthier way, regardless of what their money story might be.

Before we go deeper here, I'd like to remind you that I am not a psychologist or a therapist. This is probably a good thing because I talk more than I listen, but I do not need a medical degree to understand that money is often a deeply triggering and emotional subject for many online entrepreneurs. Since 2014, I've spent almost every working day talking to successful online business owners about their money. We are talking thousands of conversations across hundreds of people running six-, seven-, and even eight-figure online businesses. I have also looked deeply into their financial reports as their businesses have thrived as well as when they have struggled. I have also had glimpses into their personal finances and seen entrepreneurs build tremendous wealth as well as squander it. All this to say, I know an unhealthy money story when I see one.

This chapter would be a big-time bummer if I told you that we had to simply accept our money stories for what they are and that our relationships with money are all doomed forever. Luckily for all of us, that is not the case.

So much of the work you are going to do while reading this book will be to help you separate your emotional self from your financial self. This way, no matter your money story, you can have a game plan for how to make more sound and profitable decisions in your online business.

Before I break down the components that make up your money story, I want to share an experience I had with a client that changed the way I think about the emotional side of money forever.

In 2019, one of our Evolved Finance clients (let's call her Sam) asked me to speak at a live event she was hosting for the customers in her group coaching program. When the time came for Sam to introduce me to the group so I could deliver my presentation, she told the audience a story that caught me completely by surprise. She proceeded to reveal to a room full of entrepreneurs that before she started working with my firm, she felt insecure and ashamed about how she managed the money in her online business. This part did not surprise me because I have heard this same sentiment from other clients over the years. What did catch me off guard was when she also admitted to the attendees that before her first coaching call with me, she had broken into tears. She must have dried her eyes well before we jumped on video because I had no idea. At the time, she had a successful six-figure business that would eventually grow into a seven-figure business. She always came across as a strong, confident, and calculated person, so I would have never guessed that her money story would have brought up so much emotion for her.

Sam's story stuck with me for weeks. She helped me realize that the money conversations I have with our clients at Evolved Finance might seem mundane to me (especially with how often I talk about money for my work), but they can make a lot of online business owners feel vulnerable, ashamed, or overwhelmed. Even the ones like Sam who I perceive as being so confident.

The emotional response online entrepreneurs have to money conversations does not just come out of nowhere. Their money stories are at the root of how they feel about money. After countless conversations with online business owners about their finances, it is clear to me that there are three main factors that shape our money stories:

1. Family and household influence
2. Cultural influences
3. Natural temperament

Let's take some time to understand the three factors that shape your money story so you can start to think about how these factors affect the way you make financial decisions in your business.

FACTOR 1: FAMILY AND HOUSEHOLD INFLUENCE

Whether you were raised by your biological parents, grandparents, stepparents, adoptive parents, foster parents, or other extended family members, how they talked and thought about money had a huge impact on how you talk and think about money today. Period.

This is exactly why the first question I ask the guests on my podcast is, "How was money modeled for you by your family growing up?" While it might seem like an unassuming question, the answers I receive are usually extremely vulnerable. Many of my guests have never thought about this before, but as they reflect on their past, they start to realize things like:

- Arguments in their house were often rooted around money, which made them feel stressed about dealing with money as adults.
- Money was a taboo subject that their family never talked about, which made them feel ashamed of how little they knew about how to manage their money as adults.
- A lack of financial resources in their family pushed their financial decision-making to extremes (spending every dollar they had or hoarding every dollar they made).
- An abundance of financial resources in their family made them feel ashamed or embarrassed to talk about money with other people.

Can you see the impact here? So much of how we feel about money is shaped by what we saw, heard, and felt in our family households growing up. While some of us are lucky enough to have grown up in a house where healthy outlooks on money were expressed and valuable money lessons were taught, most of us were left to absorb bad financial habits or be left in the dark about the fundamentals of smart money management.

It is important to remember that your caretakers likely modeled for you what was modeled for them. Simply being aware of how your home life growing up shaped your money story can be enough to begin breaking the negative financial behaviors that were taught to you by your family. It might also open the door for you to embrace some of the positive behaviors you witnessed as well. That said, you may find it necessary to seek the help of a mental health professional to support you with processing your feelings and experiences. Especially if any childhood traumas are connected to your outlook on money.

FACTOR 2: CULTURAL INFLUENCES

Cultural influences are rooted deep in us. Our cultural background shapes our beliefs, values, customs, and behaviors. It provides us with a framework for understanding the world around us and helps us to make sense of our experiences. That same framework also has a perspective on money that we either consciously or unconsciously absorb. That is why if you talk to someone from a big city like New York or London, they will have a different view about money than someone who lives in a rural area of Georgia or Saskatchewan.

For instance, if you grew up in a big city like New York, you might feel more optimistic about your ability to make a high income due to your exposure to other wealthy people. It is not hard to meet others who have high-paying jobs or run successful businesses in a place like Manhattan, so it would be no surprise that the people who grow up there feel like making a lot of money is not a strange or foreign idea. On the flip side, if you grew up in a rural farm town where job opportunities are limited and real-world examples of wealth are hard to come by, it would make sense how that experience could make money feel like a scarce resource.

Cultural influences can go beyond just the cities and towns we live in though. There are cultural influences that we absorb from our religious communities, our racial identities, our political affiliations, and the friend groups we associate with. For better or worse, all these influences have shaped your money story. It's up to you to decide if the money stories from your cultural influences are serving you.

FACTOR 3: NATURAL TEMPERAMENT

When it comes to nature versus nurture, there is no question that our environment has a profound impact on who we are as people, but there is also no denying that we are all born with a certain amount of innate programming toward a certain disposition. Some people will naturally have a positive attitude while others tend toward looking at the glass being half empty. Some people are always ready to crack a joke while others are naturally more serious.

Whatever your natural temperament is, it affects your outlook on money. While money mindset and financial habits can be reshaped over time, we are all born with personality traits that put us somewhere on a spectrum of being spenders or being savers.

SPENDER   **SAVER**

While I do believe that some people can have natural temperaments that put them somewhere in the middle of the spender-saver spectrum, most of the online business owners I have talked to lean more heavily to one side than the other. When it comes to personal finances, being a saver would normally be preferential, but when it comes to business finances, finding a middle ground is crucial.

For instance, I have worked with online entrepreneurs who are so afraid to spend money that they stunt the growth of their businesses because they are not willing to take on expenses that will help them to attract new customers, service more customers, or help to improve their operations. Does the lack of spending help their profit margins? Sure. But it also stops them from building a business that can generate larger amounts of revenue.

On the flip side, I have also worked with many online business owners who are always spending money at a rate that is not sustainable for their profits. Some of those investments might help to grow the top line sales of the company, but as you will learn later in this book, growth with no regard to profit creates missed opportunities to build your wealth as the owner, plus it makes your online business far riskier and more stressful to operate.

••••••

I have some good news and bad news for you.

The bad news is that I cannot go back in time and change your money story. The good news is that you do not have to let your money story shape your mindset on how you manage the money in your online business. To prevent that from happening, you first need to bring an awareness to how your emotions around money are affecting the decisions you make in your business.

Let's talk about mindfulness for a second. Mindfulness is a mental state where you are able to acknowledge and bring awareness to your feelings, thoughts, and emotions without judging them. When you feel a strong negative emotion rise within yourself, whether you realize it or not, you have a choice to express that emotion in a healthy way or in an unhealthy way. The thing about being human is that emotions can overtake our ability to think logically, which can cause many people to act impulsively, especially when they are feeling negative emotions like frustration, fear, or anger.

Cultivating mindfulness in yourself allows you to develop a deeper awareness of your emotions so you can be conscious of what you are feeling in any given moment. This focused awareness of your emotions does not change the way you feel, but it does give you a fighting chance to choose a healthier and less impulsive response to whatever emotion you are feeling.

This leads us back to your money story. If the three factors we discussed earlier in this chapter shape your money story, and your money story affects the way you feel about money when you work in your business, then one of the best things you can do for yourself is to reflect on your money story. Doing so will not only help you understand why you feel the way you do about money, but it will also help you to develop awareness around the emotions that might be stopping you from addressing the financial side of your business.

To help you better reflect on your own money story, I've compiled a list of questions to ask yourself. You can write out your answers in a journal, discuss them with your therapist, or talk through them with trusted friends or family members. All that matters is that you are taking the time to dive into your money story so you can better understand how it has shaped the way you make decisions with money.

- How was money modeled in your household by your parent(s)/caretaker(s) growing up?
- Was money a source of tension for your family? Did you witness arguments and fights about money?
- Did your parent(s)/caretaker(s) have direct conversations with you about how to manage money?
- Was money a taboo subject that you were discouraged from discussing?

- Did you see your parent(s)/caretaker(s) make decisions around money that you disagreed with? If so, why?
- How do you think your homelife affected the way you feel about money today?
- What is the general outlook on money in the country/state/city/town you grew up in? Do you think it has affected the way you think about money?
- What is the culture around money like within your ethnic, religious, political, and hobby/interest communities? Do you share the same outlook on money as these communities?
- Do you consider yourself a "numbers person"? Why or why not?
- Do you have or have you ever had a system for tracking your personal spending? Why or why not?
- Do you value freedom or security more? Why? How do you think this affects the way you manage your money?
- Where do you think you land on the spender-saver spectrum? Why?
- Are you someone that worries about not having enough money? Why or why not?

• • • • • •

The way we handle our personal finances is different from how we handle our business's finances. Our personal financial decisions are rooted in so much emotion, ego, and preference that, as I mentioned before, it would be completely reasonable to work with a therapist to help you address your money mindset.

Your business is a different beast. You can make tremendous progress in how you manage its money even if you have a less than ideal personal money story. You can accomplish this by removing the opportunity for emotions to be a factor in how you manage your finances. There are three things you need to do to make this happen:

1. Track the flow of money in your business so you have financial visibility.
2. Look at your numbers on a regular basis so you are not in the dark on your business's financial health.
3. Disconnect your business's finances from your personal identity.

I understand that these three actions will make many of you want to roll your eyes into the back of your heads. It is the financial equivalent of your dentist telling you to floss more or your doctor telling you to eat healthier. Regardless, I am asking you to bear with me for a page or two because the logic behind these three actions can be a game changer for dealing with the emotional side of your business's finances.

The first thing you need to understand is that your numbers do not lie. They deliver truth, and you can never get enough truth as a business owner. The clearer you see the realities of your business, the more focused and precise action you can take to grow your business in a healthy way. If you cannot see the truth of your online business's finances, then you are doomed to run your business based on feelings and emotions alone. This is not only a risky way to run any sort of business, but it is also emotionally draining. The more connected you are with the true and unbiased realities of your online business, the less room for your money story to sneak in and complicate things. To obtain more financial truth from your business, you need to have better systems for tracking how money is moving in and out of your bank accounts. Not to worry. We'll teach you how to create these systems in the chapters ahead.

Once you have better financial systems in your online business, then your truth will come in the form of financial reporting. I really wish there was another term for financial reporting, because if we called these reports money porn, more online business owners would be looking at their numbers each month, but I digress. Your financial reports are the result of your financial systems working their magic to organize and track the money in your business. The point of these reports is to deliver the clear and honest truth of how financially healthy your business is. The type of truth that no business coach or consultant can compete with. The only problem is most online business owners do not want to look at them.

Do you remember how scary it was to be in a dark room as a kid? Hell, many adults still get creeped out being alone in their homes at night. The reason most children fear the dark is because their imaginations run wild with what could be hiding in the shadows. The same goes for the money in your business. If you avoid looking at any sort of financial reporting in your business, you are keeping yourself in the dark about the truth of your financial situation, which opens the door for your imagination to fill in the unseen areas of your business with fear, shame, and any other emotions you have tied to your money story.

For a lot of online business owners, there are some valid reasons why they are not looking at their financial reports. They might not have financial systems in place that allow them to generate reports of any kind. Or perhaps they do not know how to interpret their financial reports, so they do not feel it is worth the time to look at them. For our clients at Evolved Finance, these are nonissues because we provide a great financial support system, organized financial data, and guidance for how to read and interpret their financial reports. Yet I still come across clients who struggle to get themselves to look at their numbers each month because they are afraid of how they are going to feel when they see the truth.

Many years ago, I discovered a trick to help these clients change the way they think about their numbers so they are able to look at their business's finances with less emotion.

The trick is to stop thinking of the money in your online business as being *your* money. Until you transfer money out of your business bank account and into your personal bank account, it is your business's money. Seeing your business as a financial entity that is separate from yourself leaves less room for your money story to get in the way of making sound business decisions. The financial decisions in your business are not about *you*, they're about doing what's right for the business. It just so happens that what's right for your business will very often benefit your personal financial situation as well.

The best way I have found to drive this point home is to envision being the CEO for a business that is exactly like yours, except you do not own the company. As the new CEO of this company, this means you are responsible for keeping the business financially healthy. How would your perspective on the numbers change in this situation? For many of the online business owners I have coached, a light switch goes on for them when they imagine this scenario. Taking on a CEO role without being the owner of the business suddenly takes the emotions out of the numbers. If anything, the clients I have done this thought experiment with say they would feel a greater responsibility to monitor the finances because they would not want to let the business owner down. This is why career CEOs are not knocking on the doors of personal development coaches trying to get help with their money mindsets. They do not connect their money stories to the finances of the business because the money in the business is not theirs to spend on themselves.

Mindset stuff is tricky. Some of you will have more work to do in this area than others. That said, with some better visibility into your business's finances and some clearer boundaries between your business and personal finances, you can do a lot to overcome your money story and strengthen your ability to make more strategic financial decisions for your online business.

• ACTION ITEMS •

Not every entrepreneur struggles with their money story as it relates to their online business. If you are one of those people who does not, consider yourself fortunate. If you are one of the many other people who feels like you have more work to do on your money mindset, then here are some ways you can dive into your money story more deeply.

- If you believe that you have trauma around money, consider finding a licensed therapist to help you work through those feelings and experiences.
- If you are already working with a trusted mental health professional, consider talking to them about your money story to see if they can help you gain a deeper understanding of your feelings and experiences.
- Review the money story questions from this chapter and answer them in a journal or Word document.
- Find and work with a coach who specializes in supporting their clients with money mindset issues.
- Schedule some time with a colleague or friend to talk about your money stories together.

Any extra work you can do to develop a deeper awareness of how money makes you feel will only help to serve you in making more unbiased and data-driven decisions in your online business down the road. Just remember that much of the work you will be doing in the subsequent chapters will greatly improve your ability to build a profitable online business, even if you have more work you want to do on your relationship with money.

3

The Two Financial Games of Online Entrepreneurship

I am an impatient person. I do not like waiting for anything that I am excited about. So much so that as a child, I would get awful stomach-aches about a week out from Christmas. Waiting for Christmas Day was a torture that my nine-year-old body just could not handle. While adulthood has brought with it a maturity that no longer leaves my body in physical pain in anticipation for the holidays, I am still impatient. I like getting to the point as soon as possible. As a busy online entrepreneur, I can imagine you feel the same way at times.

It would be easy for me to dive into the financial tactics you have been waiting to read about in this book right now, but I think it is important that you and I are on the same page about a larger, overarching business concept before we go down that road: the two games of an online business.

For many online entrepreneurs, it is easy to learn about a new business strategy, only to lose momentum on the execution of said strategy a few weeks or months down the road. Most often, this happens because the business owner does not have a clear vision for how this new strategy is going to help their business in the long term. Is the work they are doing to integrate the new strategy going to deliver a worthwhile result later? If the business owner does not fully buy into the payoff they will receive from their efforts, then they are not going to show up and do the work.

I would hate for this to be your experience after reading this book. Getting your finances right is too important for the future of your business. I want you to internalize the greater vision you have for the financial health of your business so you can give yourself the motivation you need to make improving your online business's finances a top priority.

To help you understand the greater vision of why upleveling the way you manage your money is so important, I am going to share with you the two games you are playing as an online business owner:

Game #1: The revenue game.

Game #2: The cash flow game.

You may not even realize you're playing these two games, but the sooner you understand the rules as well as the tactics and strategies you must adopt for winning at them, the closer you will get to a profitable business. And the sooner you recognize you must play both games, the more urgency you will have to uplevel your financial understanding of your online business.

Game #1 is all about generating revenue. Every business needs to make sales if they want to survive in the market. Without paying customers, an online business becomes an expensive hobby. You might be busy working on landing pages, writing emails, making content for social media, and developing new offers, but if you are not selling anything, your business will fail. Seems obvious enough, right?

So, it is no wonder that there are thousands upon thousands of coaches, consultants, software companies, and agencies dedicated to helping businesses generate more revenue. Whether their online business is brand new or they've been in business for years, every entrepreneur wants more revenue. With that revenue comes the flexibility to invest back into the business or pay yourself a larger salary, so it is only natural that business owners focus on Game #1 as much as possible.

For new online entrepreneurs, Game #1 is even more important because their baseline revenue is $0. Getting that first sale or having that first month of $1,000 in revenue is a crucial first step toward building an online business that can make even more money in the future. Online businesses at this level are testing their offer(s), honing their marketing messaging, and finding any way possible to get in front of their potential customers. Almost the entirety of their business activity revolves around driving sales because their business is in survival mode.

Here is the trap though. The importance of Game #1 in the early stages of your business can trick you into thinking that the only thing you need to worry about for the rest of your business's existence is to drive revenue. The idea being that if you have more and more customers pulling out their wallets to pay for your offer(s), then the profitability stuff will fall into place on its own. I wish this were the case, but it is simply not the reality of business.

As your revenue grows, so will your expenses. I do not care how cost conscious you are, if you want your business to grow, then you will need to take on more expenses along the way. What most online business owners underestimate is just how quickly those expenses can build up. This is where Game #2 begins.

Game #2 revolves around managing the flow of money in and out of your business, also known as cash flow management. The goal of this game is to ensure that your online business is making more money than it is spending so it can turn a profit. In order to do this, the business owner's ability to manage their expenses needs to be as strong as their ability to drive revenue.

Let's drive this home with a simple formula. As seen below, profit is calculated by taking your total revenue and subtracting out the business expenses. The money left over is your profit.

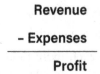

Revenue

- Expenses

Profit

Playing Game #1 involves making your revenue numbers as big as your business can handle. The focus of Game #2 is to ensure that your business expenses do not grow as quickly as your revenue. If you can play both of these games well, then your reward will be a profitable online business.

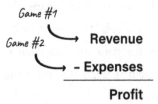

Revenue

- Expenses

Profit

Let's put some numbers to this formula and show you how a lot of online entrepreneurs get sucker punched by Game #2.

In the example that follows, this online business has generated $75,000 in revenue. The business expenses are $15,000, which, when subtracted out from the revenue, leaves the business with a profit of $60,000. This level of profitability would be awesome for an online business of this size.

Revenue	$75,000
- Expenses	$15,000
Profit	$60,000

If this same business wanted to double its revenue next year, they would simply forecast out $150,000 as their revenue and expect the expenses to stay the same. This scenario is shown below.

Revenue	$150,000
- Expenses	$15,000
Profit	$135,000

Would it be impossible for an online business of this size to double their revenue while keeping their expenses exactly the same as the previous year?

No.

Is it unlikely?

Yes.

With this much revenue growth, the business owner would likely need to support this growth by investing in their team, software, continuing education, or marketing expenses. Their accountant might also suggest new tax strategies that will help reduce the business owner's tax bill, but will create additional expenses for the business as well.

A more realistic representation of the business would look like the example on the next page.

Revenue	**$150,000**
- Expenses	**$50,000**
Profit	**$100,000**

Notice how the expenses increased quite a bit? They went from $15,000 to $50,000. This is a significant jump, but not an unreasonable one. For any business to be able to generate $150,000 in revenue and keep $100,000 of it as profit is a huge win, but it sure does not look as nice as the $135,000 in profit in the previous example. This is the lesson that Game #2 has to offer. Do not underestimate how quickly your business expenses can increase as your revenue grows.

• • • • • •

A lot of online business owners look at a $1,000,000 revenue year as a tremendous milestone in their careers. In fact, you may have even seen other online business owners humblebrag on social media about crossing the seven-figure threshold in their own businesses. Or maybe you have paid for a business course or coaching program where the business owner uses their own seven-figure business as a credential for their expertise. Any business that can sell a million dollars' worth of anything has accomplished an impressive revenue goal, but with your newfound knowledge of the two games we play in our online businesses, I am hoping you can understand that revenue accomplishments do not tell the full story of a business's success and health. It does tell you that they're pretty good at playing Game #1, but it does not guarantee that they are any good at playing Game #2.

Let me use some numbers to show you what I mean.

Imagine two identical online businesses that both generated $1,000,000 in revenue last year selling the exact same offers. The owners are obviously accomplished at playing Game #1, but as you will see from their financial reports below, only one of them has learned the importance of skillfully playing Game #2.

If you look at the financial report for Business A, the first thing that should jump out at you is how much this business spent on advertising. The $800,000 they spent on ads makes up 80% of their total revenue for the year. It would be safe to assume that the owner of this business had a goal of hitting $1,000,000 in sales for the year and was willing to do whatever it took to get there. In this case, that meant spending money on social media advertising to reach as many new customers as possible, despite the effect that spending had on their profits. When you look at the bottom of Business A's financial report, you can see that company only had a profit of $50,000. While $50,000 is a not a small amount of money, I can assure you that if you had to deal with the stress and pressure of building a seven-figure online business, a profit margin of that size would leave you feeling disappointed.

BUSINESS A

Revenue	**$1,000,000**
Advertising	**$800,000**
Team Expenses	**$100,000**
Operating Expenses	**$50,000**
Total Expenses	**$950,000**
Profit	**$50,000**

More on Business A in a moment. Let's now look at Business B.

Right off the bat, you can see that this business spent only $300,000 on advertising, but they were still able to generate $1,000,000 in sales.

This could have been due to several factors, but ultimately, Business B was more strategic with their marketing efforts and was able to get a much better return on investment from their ad spend. By spending so much less on their advertising expenses, Business B was also able to invest more money into their team expenses as well as into their operating expenses. Even with these two expense categories being higher than Business A's expenses, Business B was able to generate a profit of $300,000. This is what most online business owners would hope to see with a business of this size. That is life-changing money.

BUSINESS B

Revenue	$1,000,000
Advertising	$300,000
Team Expenses	$250,000
Operating Expenses	$150,000
Total Expenses	$700,000
Profit	$300,000

There are a few other assumptions we can make based on these two financial reports.

1. Business A had a much smaller budget for team and operating expenses because they had to spend so much money on ads. This likely led to the business owner doing much more of the work in the business themselves because they could not afford to hire more people to help them run the business. So, not only were their profits low, but they were likely dealing with burnout and work-life balance issues as well.

2. Business B's ability to invest in their team and operating expenses likely means they had the support they needed to take care of their customers and give them a great experience. It also means the business owner was able to strike a better work-life balance because they could afford the team and systems needed to scale a seven-figure business in a healthy way. So, not only did they turn a great profit, but the business has the support it needs to scale sustainably.

Business B did a much better job of playing Game #2. They were more strategic and thoughtful about how they spent their money, which allowed them to grow their revenue without sacrificing their profit as well. For an online business of this size, it is easy to see in the numbers of these two companies how managing cash flow and expenses becomes just as important as their ability to generate revenue.

· · · · · ·

If your online business generates any amount of profit, you are in rare company. Most aspiring entrepreneurs talk about wanting to start a business and then never see a single cent of revenue hit their bank accounts. Even if you are barely making enough money to cover the cost of your software each month, you are accomplishing what most people never will. Congrats!

Eventually, every entrepreneur needs to graduate to a more strategic mindset if they want to have consistent and stable incomes that they can rely on for years to come. Whether your online business is your full-time income already or you are aspiring to quit your day job, you need to think beyond your sales and marketing (Game #1). Of course it never hurts to make more money, but as you have learned in this chapter, if you are not being strategic with how you invest in your business along the way

(Game #2), you could very easily hit major revenue milestones and see very little financial benefit from those efforts.

So, this all begs the question—how do you get better at playing Game #2?

Gain visibility into your money.

As you will learn by the end of this book, understanding your numbers is one of the easiest parts of running an online business. There are so many other parts of running your business that take far more specialized problem-solving and creative thinking than just looking over a basic financial report. I am serious! Writing copy, creating content, developing offers, and even customer service demand skills that take years of practice to develop. You can drastically improve your financial literacy and the financial systems in your business in a matter of weeks or months. Once you have this knowledge, it will serve you for the rest of your entrepreneurial career.

So why are more online business owners not aware of and comfortable with their finances? Because they can't see what the hell is going on! I have talked to more online business owners than I can count about their financial woes, and the most common issue is they have no numbers to look at. They are getting zero feedback from their business about what is working and what is not working financially.

Let me paint a picture of why financial visibility is so important.

Imagine I give you a brand-new car. Before you thank me, know that there is a catch. When you sit in the driver's seat so you can take in that new car smell, you quickly notice that there is no dashboard behind the steering wheel. That means no speedometer, no odometer, no fuel gauge, no tire pressure light, and no check engine light. The car still turns on and functions normally, but you have no feedback about the status or health of the vehicle for as long as you drive it.

How do you feel about your new car now?

You obviously cannot just turn down a free car, even one as quirky as this one, so you decide to suck it up and make this dashboard-less car your new daily driver. Depending on your personality type, you have two options for how you can handle this less-than-ideal driving experience.

If you are like me, you will be an absolute anxious mess driving this car around town. You will be going to the gas station more than you need to because you will always be afraid of running out of gas. You will waste hours of time at the mechanic getting unnecessary oil changes and maintenance done because you will be worried that there are mechanical issues that your car is not telling you about through the dashboard. On top of all this, you won't ever know how fast your car is going, leaving you prone to getting speeding tickets. Or perhaps the fear of a speeding infraction leans you toward wasting your time driving under the speed limit for every trip, forcing you to leave earlier than normal every time you drive.

There is another end to this spectrum. Maybe you are the type of person that is going to drive this car with reckless abandon, having no worries about the unknown and no concerns about the "what-ifs." While I do admire this less neurotic outlook on driving this car, it does not free you from the repercussions. The biggest one being the amount of time and money you would waste as your car is towed to the mechanic after running out of gas on the highway or from an engine problem that a car with a normal dashboard would have alerted you about weeks before. You would also collect your fair share of speeding tickets as you guessed how fast you were driving on every road you went down.

Waiting for your dashboard-less car to billow smoke from under the hood or make weird rattling sounds as it idles at a stoplight is no better as a strategy for taking care of the vehicle than anxiously over-maintaining your car as you bite your nails and breathe into a paper bag. Both options objectively suck. To the point that it would be reasonable to question if all the headaches this car comes with are even worth the lack of a monthly car payment.

Do you understand where I am going with this somewhat heavy-handed metaphor? Running an online business with no financial visibility, no financial dashboard, and no financial feedback is not a sustainable way to operate a company. You can get away with it for a little while, but as your business grows, the cost of not seeing financial issues creeping into your business can be devastating.

In addition, I cannot emphasize enough how much financial visibility can have a positive impact on your confidence and stress levels as a business owner. After all, knowledge is power. When you have the data and information you need to better understand how your online business functions, you are left feeling far more empowered. You can sleep better at night knowing that there are not any unforeseen issues creeping into your business. Even if your numbers are not ideal, would you not feel better knowing where you need to focus your attention to fix those issues instead of guessing what needs to be done?

Gaining financial clarity does not mean you need to hire an expensive CFO or enroll in an MBA program. Far from it. You will need to build better financial processes and systems, know the right experts to hire for the financial tasks that do take specialized knowledge, know which financial tasks you and/or your team can manage, and then make reviewing your numbers each month as much a part of your business as maintaining your sales funnel or serving your customers.

· · · · · ·

I do not know about you, but I like to see the big picture before I dive into the details of any project in my business. If I can get a macro-level view of what I am trying to accomplish, I can dive into the details with more gusto. That is why I want to lay out the plan of attack for the next seven chapters so you can see how this book's framework will provide you with the financial foundation you need to build into your online business so you can become a badass at playing Game #2.

In order to build a sturdy financial foundation for your online business, you will need to focus on five key areas. In my opinion, these are nonnegotiable. If you are missing even one of these five components, you jeopardize your ability to have the financial clarity you need to effectively play Game #2. Please note that each of these five key areas will be discussed in more detail in parts two and three of the book.

CLEANING UP YOUR PERSONAL FINANCES

It may seem counterintuitive, but the first step toward strengthening your business's financial foundation is to clean up your personal finances. If you do not know how much money you need to make personally to live, then you are going to have a hard time setting clear financial goals for your business. Plus, most online entrepreneurs underestimate how much their personal financial situation can drain their business's bank account, thereby significantly reducing their business's financial flexibility. So, by putting some time and focus into understanding (and cleaning up) your personal finances, you put yourself in a stronger position to make smart financial decisions for your online business. We will dive into this more deeply in chapter four.

UNDERSTANDING THE FINANCIAL FUNCTIONS OF YOUR BUSINESS

Another important step toward strengthening your financial foundation is learning about the different financial functions in your online business. Part of what makes the financial side of running an online business stressful for so many people is the lack of clarity around how your finance department should function. When you have an appreciation for what these functions are, why they are important, and who should be responsible for managing them, your confidence as a business owner will skyrocket because you will no longer have a large part of your business that makes you feel insecure and/or uninformed. Chapter five delves into everything from bookkeeping, taxes, and all of the other primary financial functions inside of your online business.

SIMPLIFYING YOUR FINANCIAL ACCOUNTS

A strong financial foundation cannot exist without simplified financial accounts. Your financial accounts consist of your business checking accounts, credit cards, merchant accounts, checkout software, and more. Having more of these accounts than you need makes everything about managing the money in your online business more difficult and confusing. It is also important to keep your business accounts separate from your personal bank accounts and credit cards. If you want a surefire way to make your accountant and bookkeeper despise you, then open eight checking accounts and mix your business and personal expenses into all of them. I lay out everything you need to know about building your financial foundation in chapter six.

UNDERSTANDING THE IMPORTANCE
OF PROFITABILITY

The entirety of this book is dedicated to helping you build a more profitable online business, so if you do not possess a deep understanding of what profit is, why it is important, and how it will benefit you and your online business, then a core piece of your financial foundation will be missing.

Profit is such a simple and powerful concept, but it is viewed differently by different business models. Your financial foundation will demand that you understand the role profit plays in accomplishing both your business and personal financial goals. You will learn all of this in chapter seven.

LEARNING HOW TO ORGANIZE
YOUR BUSINESS EXPENSES

The most important component to mastering Game #2 is having clear financial reporting that is easy for you as the business owner to understand. To do this, your business expenses need to be tracked and organized in a manner that offers real insight into how money is flowing in and out of your business. That is why the last step you need to take toward strengthening your financial foundation relies on understanding the four profit pillars that live in your online business. Once you understand how to categorize your expenses into these four profit pillars, as well as how much you can spend in each of these pillars without destroying your profitability, your financial vision will be 20/20. Chapters eight, nine, and ten will lay this all out for you.

· · · · · ·

Finance has a way of feeling scarier and more complicated than it actually is. As someone who spent years of his life not feeling like a numbers person, I can relate to this more than you know. Luckily, small business finance is not nearly as difficult as you might have built it up in your head. I say this because if just reading about the five components of your financial foundation makes you feel overwhelmed already, please know that we will walk through all these foundational components one step at a time. I've been teaching online business owners about all these things since 2014 and have seen them achieve great success. I know you can too.

PART 2
Building Your Financial Foundation

The following three chapters focus on cleaning up your financial house (both personally and in your business). Every person reading this book will benefit from doing the work suggested in these next chapters. I know this because I have seen very successful online businesses let their finances get disorganized and messy. This is usually because they did not build their business on a simple, clean, and scalable financial foundation to begin with. If you want to get the most out of the Profit Pillars system, then you have to build a solid and stable financial foundation for your business. These next three chapters will show you exactly how to do that.

4

The Hidden Impact of Your Personal Finances

One of the most common questions I get asked by online business owners is, "How much should I pay myself?" My response is extraordinarily unsatisfying because I ask them a question of my own.

"How much money do you *need* to make?"

Annoying, right?

Regardless of how much money your online business is making, you have a certain amount of personal expenses each month. These are things like your rent or mortgage, car payment(s), student loan payment, groceries, and household items, just to name a few.

As an online business owner, you have four main ways you can pay your personal bills. With money you have:

1. Earned from your business.
2. Earned from another income source like a part-time or full-time job, investments, or from your spouse's income.

3. Saved in a personal savings account.

4. Borrowed through a credit card or personal loan.

I do not need to be a mind reader to know that you probably want to pay your personal bills with money earned entirely from your business. If you are already there, then congratulations. If you are not quite there yet, keep fighting the good fight. Either way, the importance of knowing how much you need to make is vital.

It should not be a surprise when I tell you that most online business owners do not have a firm grasp of how much money they need each month to pay their personal bills. Subsequently, they use their businesses like ATMs. When they see money in their business checking account, they transfer it to their personal checking account whenever they need to cover a personal expense. There is absolutely nothing wrong with doing this because the purpose of your online business is to support your life-style, but when your personal financial needs are constantly draining your business of cash, you will always be left wondering why it feels like your business never has any money left over at the end of the month.

That is why I want to take some time in this chapter to focus on your personal budget. I understand that this is a book about mastering your online business's finances, but there are a handful of reasons why I want to start with your personal finances before we dive into your business's finances.

- Managing your personal budget isn't that different from managing the money in your online business, so taking some time to focus on cleaning up your personal finances is a great warm-up for looking at the numbers in your business.
- Your personal financial situation has a big impact on your business's cash flow. Maximizing your personal budget will help to

free up money in your online business so you have the flexibility to invest in its growth.

- Having clear personal financial goals will help you be more intentional in building an online business that can support those goals.

- No matter how profitable your online business is, if you do not have a grasp of your personal finances, to the point that you never have money to save or invest for retirement, you will miss out on the primary way your business can help you build wealth.

Integrating a personal budget into your financial habits is game changing. So much so that one simple budgeting spreadsheet changed the trajectory of my entire financial life. I know it sounds overdramatic, but that does not make it less true. Allow me the opportunity to over-share for a bit.

· · · · · ·

Shortly after I graduated from college in 2004, I found a full-time office job that paid 11 dollars per hour. Like most people in their early 20s, I lived paycheck to paycheck. For my situation, I am willing to cut myself some slack because, even for 2004, 11 bucks per hour was barely a livable wage. I also lived in Los Angeles, where the cost of living is higher than most other cities in the country. By 2005, I was poached by a small automotive consultant who increased my hourly wage to 14 dollars per hour. This was the best hourly wage I had ever been paid at this point in my life. Surely, I would be able to start saving money now, right?

Wrong.

I stayed at the automotive consultant company for five years. Those last couple of years I was making 20 dollars per hour. That felt like pretty good money for a musician with a day job. Did I mention I was playing in a rock band at night? Despite my raises over those five years, I am sure you will be unsurprised to hear that I was still living paycheck to paycheck. My expenses always seemed to keep pace with my income bumps. Not that I was paying attention to any of this because I was not tracking how I was spending my money in the slightest. If all my bills were paid before I ran out of money at the end of the month, I was good to go. If I had an unexpected expense like a car repair or medical situation, I was screwed.

My band would eventually break up around 2008, which opened the door for me to explore a career change. And by opened the door, I mean I was thrown over the threshold headfirst. I decided to move back down to San Diego (my hometown) and live with my parents for a year so I could figure out my next move. The owner at the automotive consultancy I was working for was kind enough to let me work from home if I was willing to be in the Los Angeles–based office once a week. I gladly took this offer.

Aside from my identity as a musician being shattered and my ego being bruised from having to live with my parents (to be fair, my parents are awesome roommates), this period of my life was a chance to reset. One of the areas that I wanted to reset was my personal finances. My parents did ask that I put some money toward utilities and food while I was living with them, but not having to spend a combined $1,100 per month on rent, utilities, and food like I did when I was living in Los Angeles was a godsend. I wanted to make sure I took advantage of my low monthly expenses so I could pay off some debt and build some savings. To help with this, I created a spreadsheet to examine my monthly financial situation.

Life. Changing.

When I say I created a spreadsheet, we are talking the simplest form of a budget possible. I had very little experience in Excel at that time, but I did know how to create basic addition and subtraction formulas, which was all I needed to get the insights into my money that I wanted. It looked something like what you see below.

Income	$2,300
Rent	$250
Auto Insurance	$150
Groceries	$200
Health Insurance	$200
Gas	$150
Entertainment	$100
Restaurants	$100
Student Loan	$150
Total Expenses	$1,300
Savings	$1,000

When I saw the number at the bottom of the spreadsheet show $1,000 a month in savings, my jaw dropped. To go from living paycheck to paycheck to saving almost half of my monthly income gave me a dopamine hit that no spreadsheet has ever matched. I suddenly saw a future where I could create some financial security, even on a modest income.

I knew these numbers were temporary though. I would eventually move into a one-bedroom apartment with my then-girlfriend (now wife) where my rent would double and expenses like my groceries, utilities, and household items would all go up as well. Despite that being the case, I was still able to save about $500 per month because my budget helped me to stay disciplined in my spending. As my wife and I made more money over the years, our budget got a little more sophisticated and the expenses in the spreadsheet got a little bit bigger. No matter what our income was, though, we were always saving money for our nest egg and for retirement. This had zero chance of happening if not for our spreadsheet.

The budget aside, another big mental breakthrough for me was seeing the money in my savings account grow. For my entire young adult life, I had never saved a penny. Now that I had money in the bank, I felt the desire to grow my savings only get stronger. Throughout my career, regardless of whether I was saving $200 per month or $2,000 per month, watching my savings account build over time was a game changer. That nest egg allowed me and my wife to always have the money we needed for unexpected car repairs, deposits on our first two apartments, down payments for houses and cars, semi-frequent vacations, and even to pay for our wedding (to be fair, it was a really small wedding). Our savings also allowed me to take a massive pay cut and jump into the world of entrepreneurship to build Evolved Finance with Corey. If my wife and I hadn't been so prudent with our money, I would not have been able to afford to put in the sweat equity necessary to become a partner at Evolved Finance and eventually write this book.

That first budget I created helped me to set clear spending goals that made saving a priority. That meant setting limits on my spending and being disciplined with my expenses even when those around me were not always doing the same. That meant living within our means when we felt the pull to keep up with the Joneses. It wasn't always easy, and we were not always perfect in our execution, but having a spreadsheet that showed me what the reward would be for our efforts was a massive motivator. I think it could be a motivator for you too.

• • • • • •

I did not realize it at the time, but learning how to manage my household budget was not just important for my personal finances. It benefited Evolved Finance too. By keeping my personal expenses manageable, my business partner and I were able to balance increasing our salaries with making investments in the business. Evolved Finance may not have been where it is today if we had to keep taking out profit to cover my increasing personal expenses instead of investing the money back into our team, systems, and marketing.

Most online entrepreneurs miss this connection. While we do teach our clients to view their personal finances as being separate from their business's finances, that does not mean these two entities are not impacted by each other.

I have had many calls with Evolved Finance clients during which they've expressed to me that they feel like their business is thriving, but when they look in their business's checking account, cash reserves are consistently low. When I look at their profit and loss statement, I can see that their numbers back up their story. The business's expenses are super reasonable relative to its revenue, which subsequently shows a great profit margin. So how can the business have a healthy profit margin but be low on cash?

The business owner was taking out most of the profit to pay themselves.

Let's make this a bit more visual. Pretend there is an online business that made $150,000 in revenue for the year. After subtracting out $70,000 in business expenses, the profit for the company shows $80,000. This means the business kept 53% of the revenue generated for the year as profit. This is an outstanding profit margin. Despite these numbers looking so healthy, the business owner claims their business checking account is always low on cash.

Revenue	$150,000
Business Expenses	$70,000
Profit	$80,000

What this very simple profit and loss statement is not showing is something called profit distribution. In the United States, profit distribution can also be called owner's draw, owner's distribution, or dividends. These are all just financial terms that describe when a business owner takes untaxed profit out of their business to pay themselves. Profit distribution does not show up on a profit and loss statement, though, because it is not a business expense. It is just you, the owner, taking money from your business's checking account and transferring it to your personal checking account.

Now that you know about profit distribution, let's expand on the previous financial data to show how much money the business owner took out as profit distribution from their online business.

Revenue	$150,000
Business Expenses	$70,000
Profit	$80,000
Owner Profit Distribution	$75,000
Cash Left in Business	$5,000

When we look at the $80,000 profit in this business, and then subtract out the $75,000 that the owner transferred to their personal bank account as profit distributions, it is easy to see why the owner feels like cash is tight. From a cash flow perspective, the business would only have $5,000 left over in the checking account despite the profitability of the business being so awesome.

Is it wrong for this business owner to transfer almost all of the business's profit to themselves? Of course not. It is their business and their money so they can decide to transfer money to themselves whenever they please. That said, the business's lack of cash on hand makes running the business far more stressful. One bad month of sales and this business owner might find themselves struggling to pay bills personally and in the business. They have no buffer and no cushion.

So what does all of this have to do with your personal finances? What's the lesson to be learned here?

The amount of money you need to pay yourself as the owner has a direct impact on how much cash your business has available to invest in the people, systems, and marketing that will help it stabilize and/or grow.

The higher your personal expenses are, the more of your business's profit you need to transfer to yourself. The lower your personal expenses are, the more cash your business will have on hand to get through a slow sales month or make important investments that stabilize and/or grow your business so it can generate higher amounts of profit down the road. This is why locking down your personal budget can be so impactful. If you have transitioned into working on your business full-time, or are on the cusp of doing so, managing your personal finances can be just as important as managing the expenses in your business.

So what is the secret to managing the relationship between your personal finances and your business finances?

A personal budget.

· · · · · ·

Creating a personal budget is easier than ever before. Between premade spreadsheets and a myriad of budgeting software options to pick from, there is really zero excuse to not have a handle on your personal finances.

As I mentioned earlier in the chapter, creating my first personal budget changed my life. Gaining clarity around my personal finances helped me to change my financial habits for the better. It also gave me the flexibility to make financial decisions for Evolved Finance that were in the best interest of the long-term financial health of the company instead of my immediate, short-term financial needs. This sort of flexibility is what has allowed my business partner and me to balance giving ourselves raises with investing back into our company.

Whether you already have a personal budget, or this chapter is motivating you to create your first ever budget, I wanted to share some tips and strategies to help you get the most out of your budgeting experience. At the end of the day, do what works for you, but as an opinionated and stubborn finance professional, I'd like to share what I have seen work for our clients at Evolved Finance as well as what has worked for me.

THE 50/30/20 BUDGETING RULE

The 50/30/20 rule has been around for a while, and there are variations of this rule strewn about the internet, but the version of this budgeting rule that I use is:

1. 50% of your monthly income goes toward fixed expenses.
2. 30% of your income goes toward variable expenses.
3. 20% of your income goes toward savings.

The most important piece here is working toward the 20% savings. If you are doing this, then it does not really matter what the breakdown is for your expenses. That said, it is very helpful to think about your expenses as being either fixed or variable (more on what that means in just a moment).

Keep in mind, as your monthly income increases over time, so does your budget. For instance, the rent for the first apartment (one-bed, one-bath) my wife and I moved into back in 2009 was $997 per month. That was roughly 25–30% of our income. We now have a four-bedroom home with a mortgage that is less than 20% of our income, despite the mortgage payment (including insurance and property tax) being significantly higher than the rent for our one-bedroom apartment. As we have earned more over the years, we have been able to spend more as well, but the amount we allow ourselves to spend is always dictated by the 50/30/20 rule.

To understand the 50/30/20 rule, let's look at the difference between fixed and variable expenses.

Get Clear on Your Fixed Expenses (50% of Your Income)

Fixed expenses are just that—fixed. These are the expenses that typically stay the same each month or year. To reduce these types of expenses, you usually need to go through some sort of intensive process. For instance, rent is considered a fixed expense. If you want to cut back on your rent, you will have to wait for your lease to end (you could also sublet or break your lease) and then move all your belongings into a new home. While people move all the time, it is a large decision and one that involves a lot of legwork. You cannot just look at your budget and decide you are going to cut back on your rent the next day. It takes effort and time to coordinate.

Here are some common examples of fixed expenses:

- Rent
- Mortgage
- Car payment
- Car insurance
- Student loan payment
- Life insurance
- Health insurance
- Cell phone bill
- Internet
- Media subscriptions (Netflix, Spotify, etc.)
- Childcare

Fixed expenses tend to be the biggest in any budget because they consist of the biggest costs in life. Housing, transportation, student loans, and insurance can easily erode a household budget very quickly. This is why the 50/30/20 rule has fixed expenses as the largest percentage of the three at 50% of your monthly income.

Here are two things to be aware of when it comes to fixed expenses.

Fixed expenses like housing and transportation can be an ego trap. The desire to want to drive a vehicle you cannot really afford or live in an area that is outside of your budget can be intense. If your budget allows you to drive a luxury car and/or rent a condo by the beach, then more power to you, but because things like rent, mortgages, and car payments are so hard to change, looking at your budget before making decisions around these larger fixed expenses is crucial for putting yourself in a financial situation that will give you flexibility to invest in your business.

I also want to acknowledge that life is more expensive than ever. Most fixed expenses like rent, car payments, and insurance are higher than they have ever been, so you do not have to be living a luxurious lifestyle for your fixed expenses to be higher than 50%. If this is your reality, increasing your income through your online business will be one of the best ways to get your fixed expenses to 50% or less of your monthly income.

SET LIMITS FOR YOUR VARIABLE EXPENSES (30% OF YOUR INCOME)

Variable expenses are expenses that tend to fluctuate each month, even if just by a few dollars. These expenses tend to be easier to adjust because you can take immediate action to reduce or increase them. For instance, if you want to save money on your electric bill, start turning off the lights in all your rooms like you are a middle-aged dad. Want to save money on fuel? Drive less and buy a bike. Need to cut back on food costs? Cook at home more instead of eating out. I'm not saying it is easy or even reasonable to make these types of cost-cutting decisions, but the fact remains that variable expenses can be altered with less friction than fixed expenses. Most people can make huge strides with their budgets simply by assessing and putting limits on their variable expenses.

Here are some common examples of variable expenses:

- Fuel
- Groceries
- Restaurants
- Entertainment and shopping
- Household items
- Self-care
- Auto maintenance
- Water/electric/gas

Variable expenses are lifestyle expenses. It takes some discipline to set limits around these areas of your life. If I am honest with myself, my true desire is to eat sushi, steak, and pizza seven times a week. Not only would my restaurant budget be egregious, but my mercury and cholesterol levels would be through the roof. That is why, in my house, we set a monthly budget that allows us to pick up food from restaurants a couple times a week while also allowing my wife and me to have one date night each month where we eat somewhere that serves something other than burritos and burgers. We can enjoy eating out while also setting limits that stop us from blowing by our budgeting goals each month.

Setting limits on variable costs is the hardest part of any budget. You are likely doing it already even if you do not have a personal budget yet, just without the disciplined approach. Looking at how you have historically spent money on your variable expenses, and then setting realistic budgeting goals for them, is fundamental to giving yourself the best chance possible to save 20% of your income each month. Without doing so, it can simply be too easy to go overboard with late-night online shopping sprees, drink nights with friends, or those predatory in-app purchases for your favorite mobile phone game. Also, cheese. The amount of money I could spend on cheese at Whole Foods is embarrassing.

PROACTIVELY PLAN FOR SAVINGS GOALS (20% OF YOUR INCOME)

This is the payoff. Savings. If you can keep your fixed expenses and variable expenses under control, saving 20% of your income becomes possible. If you want to be more aggressive and shoot for saving 30–50%, knock yourself out. For most of us, though, we simply need to start by putting aside any amount we can afford. Maybe saving 5–10% of your income each month is where you need to start. Setting a smaller savings goal is your first step toward reaching a 20% savings goal. It does not have to be all or nothing when it comes to your budget, but as your income grows and you change your spending habits, getting to 20% should be the goal.

Building up a nest egg in your savings account is important for several reasons. While most of them are obvious, the amount of stress and anxiety you can take off your shoulders from having a healthy savings account is invaluable. Especially for entrepreneurs with incomes that can fluctuate from year to year.

The purpose of your savings account is to:

1. Have an emergency fund for unplanned expenses and changes in household income. Most financial experts recommend saving anywhere from 6–12 months' worth of personal expenses.
2. Pay for larger expenses like down payments for houses and cars or your children's college tuition.
3. Set aside money to invest.

Keep in mind that, as a business owner, you will be thinking about your personal savings account a little differently than someone who is an employee. For instance, while all entrepreneurs should have personal emergency funds, their businesses may also have cash reserves that would cover their salary for at least a few months in case their sales dipped unexpectedly, so they might not need to have as much money saved in their personal account if they have extra cash saved in their business account. Also, while all entrepreneurs should have money in safe investments like retirement accounts, they have the added ability to invest money back into their businesses and potentially see returns that are better than the stock market or real estate.

If you are serious about maximizing your personal savings, then as soon as you lay out your monthly budget, set up a monthly transfer that automatically moves money from your personal checking account to your savings account. By moving the money at the start of the month, you remove the temptation to spend the money you see left over in your checking account at the end of the month. Moving the money to savings at the start of the month makes it less accessible, which means you are more likely to only spend the money you have left over in your checking account. My wife and I have done this for years and it is a big part of why we've been able to hit our savings goals throughout our lives.

PRIORITIZE WHERE TO SPEND YOUR MONEY

One of the best thought exercises you can do around your personal finances is to get clear on your financial priorities. While we would all love to be in a financial situation that allows us to spend as much money as we want, on whatever we want, whenever we want, each of us must do the best with the financial resources we have. I do not care if you make $50,000 a year in income or $500,000 a year, you need to draw a line in the sand around what you want to spend your money on and what you do not want to spend your money on if you want to have any hope of saving 20% or more of your income each month.

So, ask yourself, what are your financial priorities? Eating high quality and healthy food? Traveling? Driving a nice car? Supporting a hobby or passion? Paying off high-interest debt? What are the areas of your life that you are willing to spend more money on than other people because it is important to you?

If you can make a list of the things you do prioritize, you might realize that you naturally deprioritize other expenses that are not important to you. If you are going to spend extra money in certain areas of your life, you will have to spend less money in other areas of your life to give yourself a chance of staying within the 50/30/20 range of your budget.

For instance, my wife and I value organic food. Since we first moved in together as a young couple many years ago, we made the decision to be okay with spending extra money on groceries so we can eat as much organic food as we can. We also value traveling. We plan a couple of trips each year and make sure our accommodations are comfortable and we have at least one nice meal in every city we visit. On the flip side, neither of us values cars. We are not attracted to luxury car brands and have never had a car payment over $350 per month despite being able to afford a higher payment. By not spending more on our vehicles, we are able to prioritize groceries and travel while still hitting our savings goals each year.

A budget does not mean you can't enjoy your life or spend money on the things you like, but there is a give-and-take. If you have a spouse or partner that you share your personal finances with, I encourage you to discuss your financial priorities together and take those into consideration as you shape your budget.

Start with a Spreadsheet

Do not overcomplicate this. Start with a spreadsheet. I know that I am biased because I dedicated a portion of this chapter to how much a single budgeting spreadsheet changed my financial future forever, but I believe the same thing can happen for you. You can graduate to budgeting software later, but for now, keep things simple and start with a Google Sheet or an Excel doc. Put your monthly personal household income at the top, all the monthly household expenses underneath the income as either a fixed or variable expense, and then subtract all the expenses from your income to see what's left over for savings each month. If you have experience with spreadsheets, then this should be one of the easiest spreadsheets you ever put together.

If you have limited experience with spreadsheets, that is not a problem either. There are a million videos on YouTube that can show you how to put together a budget. Plus, if you do not have much experience with spreadsheets, this is an opportunity to learn the basics. Spreadsheets are to businesses as oxygen is to humans: essential.

Don't want to build a spreadsheet from scratch? Or perhaps you want the same budget we give to our clients at Evolved Finance? Our digital companion course includes a budgeting spreadsheet tailored to the needs of entrepreneurs and is for sale on the Evolved Finance website.

There is no shortage of financial professionals teaching people how to master personal budgeting. I promise you won't hurt my feelings if you want to learn from someone else. All I care about is that you gain more clarity around your personal financial situation so you can have more flexibility to invest back into your business as well as build incredible wealth from all the profits your business is going to generate for you.

Use Budgeting Software

Putting together a personal budgeting spreadsheet will paint a picture of what your finances can look like if you stay perfectly on budget each month. A spreadsheet is also easy to adjust as you shape your budget for the first time or make significant changes to your finances. All of this is great, but eventually you will have to start living according to this budget. You will need to be held accountable for not spending more money than you have budgeted each month. This is where budgeting software can help.

Budgeting software is essentially bookkeeping software for your personal finances. It will help you to keep track of what you are spending money on to see if you are over or under the budget you have set for each expense category from your spreadsheet. For instance, if you set a budget of $400 per month for groceries in your spreadsheet, but your budgeting software is showing you've been spending closer to $500 per month on groceries, then it is important that you know so you can cut back on your grocery spending or increase your grocery budget and reduce what you have budgeted in a different expense category.

Managing your budgeting software does take a small commitment of time each month because you have to categorize each transaction that goes through your bank accounts or credit card accounts. We are talking less than an hour a month though. For me, I can knock out our transactions for an entire month in less than 20 minutes (especially if my wife is with me to help classify her transactions). This is a nominal amount of time for the amount of benefit you will get in return. How many of your other chores have the potential to build your wealth and make you rich? The answer is zero, unless of course you pan for gold in your backyard.

There are so many more budgeting software options available now compared to what I had access to in 2008 when I started my own budget. A quick Google search will provide you with a ton of options. Some are free while others will have a monthly or yearly fee. If you are curious about the software I recommend, you can visit the Evolved Finance website to learn more.

Talk with Your Partner

If you share your finances with a spouse or life partner, then they will have to be part of the budgeting process too. Even if you both have separate checking accounts, a personal household budget should include all revenue and all expenses for each earner. Regardless of the financial goals you have for your online business, your personal finances are about building a future for you and your significant other to share and benefit from together. That means both people getting aligned on the same financial priorities and being willing to adjust their spending habits in order to help you both reach your financial goals.

If you and your significant other do not normally talk about money, this is your chance to start the conversation. Financial disagreements are one of the leading causes for divorce in the United States, and as with most relationship issues, a lack of communication and transparency is usually a big culprit. Working on a budget with your partner puts all the cards on the table. The numbers can speak for themselves. I am not a relationship counselor, so if you need help getting the conversation started, working with a financial planner, a therapist, or personal finance coach are all great options to get more support.

▪ **ACTION** ITEMS ▪

If I could show up at your home and force you to work on your personal budget, I would. Unfortunately, the logistics of doing that would be challenging for me. I hope this chapter motivates you to create your first personal budget or refresh an old budget you have not worked on in a while. If you long for more financial security and abundance, you will struggle to achieve either of those things if you put your head in the sand and simply hope you make so much money from your online business that you never have to budget for anything at all. Being good with money is not about complicated math formulas or sophisticated investment strategies. It is about having a deeper awareness of how you are spending your money so you can be more conscious and intentional with your spending habits. A budget is the only way I know to accomplish this.

Below is a checklist of tasks to help get you well on your budgeting way. You may not need to do all of these things, but review them anyway and take what you need.

❑ **Reflect on your financial priorities and write them down.** If you have a significant other who you share your personal finances with, discuss your priorities together. Getting aligned will be important for when it comes time to set a budget for each of your expenses.

❑ **Create your personal budget in a spreadsheet with your expenses split into fixed and variable.** You can find videos online to help you create your budget in a spreadsheet. You can also purchase the companion course for this book at evolvedfinance.com, which includes a budget spreadsheet template and a video tutorial on how to use it.

❑ **If you are *not* working full-time in your online business yet, determine how much money your business needs to pay you to cover your personal expenses.** Use your budget to help you arrive at this number and be sure to take into consideration what you would owe in taxes on the income your business would provide you.

❑ **If you *are* working full-time in your business, determine the ideal amount of money you'd like your business to pay you to achieve more of your personal financial goals.** Your business might not be able to pay you this desired amount now, but it's still useful to have a goal you can work toward achieving.

❑ **If you are not currently able to save 20% of your household income, determine if there are expenses you can cut back on to get you there.** If there are not, how much would your income need to increase in order to save 20% each month?

❑ **Choose a budgeting software to help you organize and categorize your financial transactions each month.** A quick Google search will show you a variety of paid and free budgeting software options.

❑ **Add a recurring event on your calendar so you have time blocked off to update your budgeting software each month (you can also do it weekly if you prefer to do the work in smaller chunks).** A simple calendar event is an easy way to carve out dedicated time and tell your subconscious mind that your personal finances are a priority.

5

The Three Financial Functions
of an Online Business

Finance is not a very intuitive business function. Even if you have worked in the finance department for a large corporation, a massive company's financial operations will be drastically more complex than that of a small business. The size of the business is not the only factor though. The type of business can have a huge effect on its financial function as well. For instance, a manufacturing business will need to track its cost of goods and utilize the accrual accounting method. On the other hand, a marketing agency would not have to worry about inventory or cost of goods. Instead, they need good financial systems for keeping track of client invoicing and monitoring the cost centers for each client project they are working on. Also, instead of using accrual accounting, a marketing agency might be using cash basis accounting instead.

If your eyes have already rolled into the back of your head after reading words like *accrual, cash basis,* and *cost centers,* I do not blame you.

You likely did not start your online business because you were excited to work in spreadsheets, look at financial statements, and create financial systems. That is fine, but it does not mean you are off the hook for being engaged with your online business's finances.

Luckily, you do not need to know how finance works for a massive corporation like Google, or a laundromat, or your favorite local restaurant. You will probably never even need to say the words *cost center* for the entirety of your career as an entrepreneur, but you do need to learn how finance works for the type of online business you own.

Here is why.

When you do not understand the foundational elements of how finance works, you make the lives of anyone managing your financial systems miserable. This can lead to higher tax bills, higher team and operating expenses, and messy financial data that holds you back from making more profitable decisions.

Here are some examples.

Do you not understand the time-sensitive nature of getting your tax documents together for your accountant? Well, now you have a stressed-out and rushed accountant who is more likely to miss tax deductions and make mistakes on your tax return because you do not understand the importance of responding to their requests in a timely manner.

Are you telling your bookkeeper to make changes to your company's financial data that makes it more confusing and less accurate? Now your bookkeeper is more likely to make mistakes due to the extra complexity you have created, which leads to your financial reports looking messy plus being less accurate and more stressful to manage. This not only affects your accountant's ability to file your taxes accurately but also makes it more difficult for you as the business owner to make profitable financial decisions.

Are you utilizing seven different checkout software systems that your team has to log into in order to find customer info, process returns, and collect sales data? Not only will you pay your team extra money for the increased hours they spend working in your inefficient financial systems, but you will also need to hire more people than should be necessary to manage those systems as your business grows.

My goal here is not to make you feel guilty or ashamed if you relate to any of the examples I just shared. Instead, I want you to feel a sense of urgency to uplevel your financial literacy so you and your team can have less friction and stress around your financial processes and systems. So many online business owners are squandering their opportunities to build real wealth through their online businesses because they are not cultivating a deeper understanding of how finance works in their companies.

Here is what I think is important for you to understand.

Any area of your business in which you do not have a foundational understanding of how it works is a vulnerability. To be clear, I am not asking you to know the inner workings of every part of your business, because as your company grows, you will have to rely on other people's expertise along the way. That said, you do have a responsibility to understand the high-level operational components for each area of your online business so you can make sure that all of them are running smoothly. If a CEO for a publicly traded company could not adequately answer a question about any major operational component of the business, they would not remain employed for much longer.

This is why I beg you to not skip this chapter. There are so many online entrepreneurs who think they understand how finance works in their online business, but they really do not know much at all. The number of times I have had to explain the difference between a bookkeeper and an accountant to an online business owner is staggering. Again, I do not say that to shame anyone but to emphasize the fact that you should not overestimate what you think you know about the financial side of your business. It might not be hurting your ability to run your business now, but it is only a matter of time before it does.

· · · · · ·

Let's talk about the "F" word: finance. What is it and how does it work for online businesses specifically?

Finance is simply the management of money in a business or organization. That sounds easy enough, right? Well, it actually is pretty easy.

Think about it this way. In general, money can only flow through an online business in five different ways.

1. Money can flow into the business as revenue generated from sales.
2. Money can flow into the business as a loan or as other forms of credit.
3. Money can flow out of the business to pay for business expenses.
4. Money can flow out of the business to pay the owner(s) in the form of profit distributions or dividends.
5. Money can flow between the various financial accounts (checking accounts, savings accounts, credit cards, merchant accounts, etc.) in the form of transfers.

If money is flowing in and out of your business, then it is important to have systems and people in place to keep track of that money. There are two main reasons for this:

1. To make sure you are accurately representing your financial data for tax purposes.
2. To monitor the financial health of the company so you can make informed decisions to keep the business profitable.

That's it. That is the role of finance in your online business. Pay your taxes and make sure your business is generating a profit. Just do not let the simplicity here distract you from the fact that these two financial functions are extremely important. Neglecting your taxes can leave you with an unexpected tax bill that can stunt or even destroy the future of your online business. The same goes for neglecting your profitability. If you wait too long to start paying attention to your numbers, you risk taking on high-interest debt or needing to close your business down completely.

So why do so many small business owners, let alone online business owners, feel like finance has to be so complicated?

What we learn about finance in school or see on TV and social media is typically related to large corporations or start-ups with millions of dollars in funding. These types of organizations have finance departments that are dealing with complex financial problems. For instance, if you look at a typical finance department for a large corporation, they have a ton of different roles and responsibilities that 99% of small businesses will never need support with. When you have hundreds of millions, or even billions, of dollars moving through the company each year, the systems for keeping track of the money, analyzing the money, and making decisions on how to spend the money can get complicated. Tax strategies also get a lot more complex at that scale.

Your online business does not have to be this complicated. In fact, I regularly tell online business owners that the key to good financial systems is to keep them simple. There will be plenty of opportunity to add complexity later if their business grows beyond the seven-figure mark. By then, they can afford to hire a finance specialist to support them with all new complexity.

What you need to know as an online business owner is that you have three main financial functions. They are:

1. Bookkeeping
2. Tax planning and tax preparation
3. Internal financial operations

You didn't think I was going to list out these three financial functions and not go into more detail about them, did you? Of course I am. Let's learn more about what these three financial functions are and what they mean for your online business.

BOOKKEEPING

Simply put, bookkeeping is the process of reconciling and categorizing all of the transactions that occur in a business. Before I explain further, you might be wondering what the hell "reconciling" means. I am glad you asked. It is the most undervalued and misunderstood aspect of bookkeeping, to the point that I have seen many bookkeepers (outside of Evolved Finance, of course) completely ignore this very important process.

Reconciling financial data in an online business is the process of ensuring that all of the financial transactions entered into the business's bookkeeping software match up exactly with all of the transactions listed on the business's financial account statements (checking, savings, credit card, merchant accounts, etc.).

While technology has made it easier than ever to transfer the financial data from a business's financial accounts into the bookkeeping software of your choice, this does not guarantee that all of the financial data has been uploaded accurately. For whatever reason, transactions can be duplicated or missing altogether due to issues with the financial institution's website or with the actual bookkeeping software itself. Human error by your bookkeeper can compromise the accuracy of your business's financial data as well. This is why the reconciliation process is so crucial.

If someone is not reviewing the data in your bookkeeping software to ensure it matches with your business's bank statements, then you risk filing an inaccurate tax return or making important financial decisions from inaccurate reports.

Once a bookkeeper gets all of the financial transactions into the bookkeeping software and has checked to make sure the data is accurate (aka, reconciled), then the bookkeeper's next job is to group all of the transactions into their appropriate categories. These categories are things like marketing, software, merchant fees, independent contractors, and so on. Not to worry. I will share more about which categories I recommend your bookkeeper use for your online business in chapter eight.

Categorizing income and expenses can vary wildly depending on your bookkeeper. What you need to understand about categorizing financial transactions as a business owner is that the care and thought put into the categorization process matters for the following reasons.

The first reason is that it helps to make filing your taxes easier. When your accountant can quickly assess how much money your business has made for the year, as well as how much it spent on various business expenses, then they can do a better job of saving you money on taxes. Poor categorization forces them to be detectives as they try to understand how money is moving through your business, which creates more opportunity for mistakes to happen. Especially when tax season is in full force, and you are the 37th business they have filed a tax return for that week.

Proper categorization is also important for you as the business owner. When your bookkeeper uses income and expense categories that make sense for your online business, it can help you better understand how money is moving in and out of your business. Whether it is visibility into how much revenue your business is generating from its different offerings or tracking how much money is going out to pay independent contractors, there is an art to categorizing your financial transactions. If your bookkeeper is skilled in this art, looking at your numbers can be powerful and insightful.

If your bookkeeper is doing their job to keep your financial data accurate and organized, you have a financial foundation that will benefit everyone else on your team that deals with the numbers. As I mentioned before, your accountant will be able to file your taxes more efficiently and effectively, but they are not the only one to reap the benefits of your clean books. Need a personal or business loan? Clean books will increase your bank's confidence in your ability to pay back the loan. Working with a financial planner to help you build more wealth? They will definitely want a clean set of books to look over as they create your wealth strategy. Does your operations manager want to create a budget for your business? A clean set of books will help them to find the financial data they need to start building out a spreadsheet.

Here is some bad news. Most accountants and bookkeepers do not care if your income and expense categories are perfect. As long as the accountant believes the categories are "good enough" for them to file your taxes, they are not going to create more work for themselves by scrutinizing the entire bookkeeping process for your business. This is why who you hire to be your bookkeeper matters. Let's explore your options.

Choosing Your Bookkeeper

In the early stages of your business, you will likely be doing your own bookkeeping. While this is less than ideal for multiple reasons (the main one being that you likely suck at bookkeeping), it is super common for any new business owner to take on this responsibility themselves until they can afford to hire a professional. My only recommendation is that you keep track of your finances in a simple spreadsheet and not try to learn how to use bookkeeping software. Not only does spending time figuring out bookkeeping software pull you away from focusing on your most important responsibility—generating sales—but you can screw up the accuracy of your financial data far more in bookkeeping software than if you just use a spreadsheet.

Let me put it this way. A professional bookkeeper spends years doing bookkeeping every day. At best, you are doing your bookkeeping once a month (*cough* . . . or more like once a year), which is not going to be enough practice to build true competence. Luckily, when your business is on the smaller side, there are not a lot of transactions to keep track of, which also means there is not a ton of financial insight to be gained from your numbers. This is why a simple spreadsheet is completely acceptable in the beginning. If you are not sure about where to start with a bookkeeping spreadsheet, visit evolvedfinance.com. We offer a premade bookkeeping spreadsheet that will hold you over until your business grows enough to hire a bookkeeper.

Once the volume of transactions in your online business increases to the point that managing them all in a spreadsheet is no longer viable, you will need to have someone else take over the bookkeeping and move you into professional bookkeeping software. So who should you hire?

I am going to be honest with you. I want you to work with my team at Evolved Finance. Finding a bookkeeper that understands online businesses is difficult, and nobody knows how to support online businesses with their bookkeeping better than us. That said, I know that our bookkeeping service will not be a fit for everyone reading this book. Not a problem though. I want everyone to find a bookkeeper that makes sense for their business, so I am going to list out the most common bookkeeping options available and give you the pros and cons of each of these bookkeeping options so you can decide which one sounds best for your online business.

Freelance Bookkeepers

Freelance bookkeepers are one of the most common options for book-keeping support. When my business partner, Corey Whitaker, started Evolved Finance with his wife, they were freelance bookkeepers. Finding freelancers of any sort is easier than ever thanks to the internet. There are websites where you can search through thousands of freelancers with expertise in anything you can imagine. Bookkeeping is often a common area of expertise you can filter for. Just make sure they are well versed in the bookkeeping standards for the country your business files taxes in. You can also search for a freelance bookkeeper locally through Google, but unless you live in a large city, finding a bookkeeper that has any experience with online businesses will be difficult to find. It's not necessary for your freelance bookkeeper to live in the same city or state/province that your business is registered in, but I do recommend your bookkeeper be located in the same country.

Pros of Working with a Freelance Bookkeeper

- You can find a freelance bookkeeper at almost any price point to meet your budget.
- Many freelance bookkeepers only have a small stable of clients, which means each of their clients can get more attention and care.
- Freelance bookkeepers can sometimes provide more customized services in order to meet the bookkeeping needs of your business.

Cons of Working with a Freelance Bookkeeper

- Freelancer bookkeepers can vary greatly in quality. Depending on how much experience they have and what sort of standards they hold themselves to, the customer experience and quality of work can be all over the map.

- They work alone, which means they do not have any immediate support when they run into bookkeeping issues that they do not know how to fix. It also means there is nobody to do their work for them if they are sick or unable to work.

- I do not know how to say this any other way: Freelance bookkeepers can be unreliable. If they suddenly decide they do not want to freelance anymore, they can drop clients with no warning.

- If your freelance bookkeeper gets popular and takes on more clients than they can handle, their work quality can deteriorate quickly as they get overwhelmed and struggle to keep up with their workload.

A freelance bookkeeper can be a perfect option for the early stages of your business. Just remember, you get what you pay for. While there is no guarantee that a more expensive bookkeeper will deliver a higher quality service, it would be foolish to think that you are going to get perfect bookkeeping at the lower end of the pricing scale.

Accounting Firm Bookkeeper

Accounting firms are one of the most popular options for bookkeeping services because it is convenient for the business owner to have their taxes and bookkeeping all in one place. An accountant has a much harder time filing a business tax return if they do not have a clean set of books to review, which is why most firms will have at least one bookkeeper on staff so they do not have to turn down a tax client simply because the client does not have a set of books.

While most online entrepreneurs love the convenience of having their tax returns and bookkeeping managed in one place, accounting firms rarely put their focus on developing a great customer experience for their bookkeeping clients. Bookkeeping is an end to a means, and that end is making money from filing taxes. If you are going to use your accounting firm's bookkeeping service, here is what you need to be aware of.

Pros of Working with an Accounting Firm

- It can be convenient to have your accountant and bookkeeper under one roof.
- An accounting firm's bookkeepers will have the support of the accountants to help them deal with problems they cannot figure out themselves.
- Many accounting firms offer competitive pricing for their bookkeeping services in order to capture your business as a tax client.

Cons of Working with an Accounting Firm

- Most accountants make their money from filing taxes, which means they do not put a lot of focus into creating a great customer experience on the bookkeeping side.
- Accounting firms tend to only look at bookkeeping from a tax perspective, which means they categorize expenses for the sole purpose of making tax time easier for themselves. Most accountants are not thinking about if the financial data is being categorized in a way that makes sense for the business owner so they can make more profitable business decisions.
- Accounting firms are usually serving hundreds, if not thousands, of clients, which means you might not get the time and attention you want from the bookkeeping service.

I am going to be honest with you. When we bring on a new bookkeeping client at Evolved Finance, if their previous bookkeeper was part of an accounting firm, the bookkeeping is often messy and confusing. I am sure there are accounting firms out there that do great bookkeeping work, but this has not been our experience. If the convenience of having your bookkeeping and tax preparation in one place is your number one priority, then by all means, move your bookkeeping to your accountant. Otherwise, do yourself a favor and consider your other bookkeeping options before automatically handing over your books to your accountant.

Bookkeeping Firm

Bookkeeping firms are far rarer than freelance bookkeepers and accounting firm bookkeepers, but as you will see, they can be one of the best options. A bookkeeping firm isn't going to file taxes or offer tax strategy. They are going to focus entirely on the management of your financial data so you can have the financial insight you need to keep your business profitable.

Please know that I am biased about bookkeeping firms. Evolved Finance was exclusively a bookkeeping firm for almost 13 years before we finally added tax planning and tax preparation services. The only other bookkeeping service I ever referred business owners to was also a bookkeeping firm. If you are making a full-time living from your business, then finding a bookkeeping firm could very well be worth the effort to ensure your books are getting the care and attention they deserve. This is why at Evolved Finance our tax accountants do not manage our bookkeeping team. We keep our tax and bookkeeping departments separate to ensure that each group is focusing solely on their area of expertise.

Pros of Working with a Bookkeeping Firm

- Their focus is only on bookkeeping, which usually means a better-quality bookkeeping experience and more accurate books.
- They have multiple bookkeepers working together, which means they have a larger knowledge base when fixing trickier issues with their clients' bookkeeping files.
- Bookkeeping firms tend to organize their clients' financial data for the purpose of financial analysis and financial health instead of only looking at bookkeeping as a function of the tax filing process.
- A firm is going to be more reliable than a freelancer because they have multiple bookkeepers ready to jump in and support each other if someone is sick or on vacation.

Cons of Working with a Bookkeeping Firm

- Bookkeeping firms are not as affordable as some freelance bookkeepers, making it difficult for smaller businesses to afford working with a firm.
- Bookkeeping firms are less likely to create custom bookkeeping processes just for your business because they need standard procedures that all of their bookkeepers can follow.
- You will need a separate accountant since bookkeeping firms do not file taxes.

If you are not able to find a bookkeeping firm, or the one(s) you have found are outside of your budget, do not lose sleep over it. A freelance bookkeeper or the bookkeeping team at your accountant's firm could still take great care of your business if you get a positive referral or do a search online.

What to Expect from Your Bookkeeper

What makes hiring a bookkeeper so difficult is that they have expertise you yourself do not possess. If you do not fully understand how they do their work, then it can be hard to know what types of questions you should be asking the bookkeepers you interview. I've got your back though.

When it comes to hiring a bookkeeper, I have written a list of questions you should be asking any bookkeeper you interview.

1. Do you fully reconcile each of my business's financial accounts each month?

As we discussed earlier in the chapter, the reconciliation process is crucial for proper bookkeeping. It is the only way to guarantee the accuracy of the financial data you and your team look at for tax and financial analysis purposes. All major bookkeeping software builds in a reconciliation process into their platforms. If your bookkeeper is not utilizing the reconciliation process, then they are likely only categorizing transactions for their clients and not confirming that the transactions are accurate. Asking about your bookkeeper's reconciliation process, even if you do not understand the details, will give you some insight into how transparent they are about their bookkeeping processes. The reconciliation process is a pain in the butt, which is why many bookkeepers will take shortcuts that could compromise the quality of the financial data in your books. So, if your bookkeeper is vague or unhelpful when you ask about the reconciliation process, that is a red flag.

2. When should I expect my monthly financial reports?

If you are making a full-time income from your online business, then you should be receiving your financial reports from your bookkeeper every single month. If your business is still a side hustle, and there is not a lot of monthly financial activity, then it might be fine to receive your financial reports on a quarterly basis. If your bookkeeper promised you monthly financial reports, but you are not getting them within the promised time frame, that should be a red flag for you as a client. Especially if they are charging you a monthly fee for their bookkeeping service.

3. What sort of financial reports will you be sending me each month?

At the very least, your bookkeeper should be providing you with two profit and loss statements each month. One should be for the most recent month they completed, and the other should be year to date (January through the most recent month completed). Another common report to get each month from your bookkeeper is your balance sheet. While I do not personally find this to be a very helpful financial report for online business owners, it is a standard report in the financial world. Your bookkeeper gets bonus points if they deliver a financial dashboard or extra reports that help you understand your business more deeply.

4. What sort of security measures do you have in place to protect my data?

For your bookkeeper to do their job, they will need access to your business's bank accounts, credit cards, merchant accounts, loans, and so on. Whether you are giving them access to your own passwords or setting them up with their own user account, it is important that you know how they are storing that sensitive information. There are so many ways to keep data secure on a computer these days that if your bookkeeper is not, at the very least, utilizing something as basic as passwords management software for all of their clients, then it may be time to find a bookkeeper that does.

5. What do you need from me to keep the bookkeeping process running smoothly each month?

Bookkeeping is not a completely passive process for the business owner. While the bookkeeper should be managing 90–95% of the process, they will need to lean on you to get access to the things they need to do their job. That might mean helping them with transactions they do not know how to categorize or updating their access to your financial accounts. I personally believe that your bookkeeper should not be asking you to download statements for them or go into the bookkeeping software to categorize transactions for them. It is up to you to decide what you are comfortable with in terms of your involvement, but if it starts to feel like you are doing their job for them, it might be time to find a new bookkeeper.

6. What is your response time like if I have questions?

If there is a gripe I hear most often about outsourced bookkeepers, it is their lack of responsiveness. It is completely natural that you will have questions and requests in regard to your bookkeeping, so if you get the sense that your bookkeeper isn't interested in providing the particular level of customer support you're comfortable with, you will need to consider if that is something you can accept.

7. How do you collaborate with my accountant?

You should not be the middle person for your accountant and bookkeeper. While your bookkeeper should not need support from your accountant most months, tax season does demand that your accountant gets access to your books. Understanding the role your bookkeeper plays in that process is an important detail. If your accountant is your bookkeeper as well, it would still be good to get clarity from them about what the year-end process looks like from a bookkeeping perspective.

8. Do you have experience doing bookkeeping for businesses like mine?

If your bookkeeper does not understand what a membership site is, why you are paying coaches for your group coaching program, or what an affiliate expense is, then that can be problematic. Not only do you want your bookkeeper to know how to reconcile more online business–specific accounts like PayPal (not easy to reconcile, by the way) so you can trust your financial data is accurate, but you also want to feel confident that they understand what a business expense for an online business looks like so they are capturing every tax deduction you can get.

Some other good questions to ask a potential bookkeeper would be:

- How does your pricing work?
- How do I cancel my services?
- Do I have to sign a yearlong agreement?
- Do I get to keep access to my financial data if I leave?

I have seen a lot of online business owners put up with bad bookkeeping for a really long time simply because they did not know what their expectations for their bookkeeper should be. Use these questions as your chance to not just find a great bookkeeper, but set the proper expectations with your bookkeeper before the work begins. A lot of bookkeepers know that their clients have no clue what they do each month, and they take advantage of that by taking shortcuts and underdelivering on their service. Just by reading this single chapter, you will be able to hold your bookkeeper accountable far better than any of their other clients. If they do not respond well to that accountability, then it is time to find a new bookkeeper. If your copywriter, graphic designer, virtual assistant, social media manager, or any other contractor you work with can be transparent about the work they do, then your bookkeeper should be able to be as well.

TAX PLANNING AND TAX PREPARATION

Most business owners know they have to pay taxes. After all, there are only two guarantees in life: taxes and death. How delightfully morbid!

When you are an employee, taxes are fairly easy. Each time you receive a paycheck, taxes are taken out automatically. Unless you have a small real estate empire on the side or are doing tons of stock trading in the evenings, you likely will not have much extra taxable income to claim outside of your yearly pay from your employer. As an employee, you will also have a limited amount of ways to reduce your tax liability. For most people with day jobs, an experienced accountant can easily knock out their tax return in less than an hour. That is, if they even decide they want the support of an accountant at all. Most people will use software to file their taxes online or simply file manually using government forms.

Businesses owners, especially those with profitable businesses, have tax deduction opportunities that employees do not get access to. This is the cool part. The not so cool part is that small business owners are responsible for making sure they pay their taxes. There is no HR department automatically setting up their payroll and deducting their taxes from their paycheck each month. As a business owner, you are responsible for figuring all that stuff out. That does not mean you should be doing your taxes yourself; you should be ready to invest in an accountant as soon as your business starts making money, because the chances of you doing your taxes correctly yourself are slim to none.

Cool, Parker. Hire an accountant. Let them file my taxes for myself and my business. Seems easy enough.

Maybe you have not discovered this for yourself yet, but not all accountants are created equal. The more money you make, the more important it is that your accountant is not just filing your taxes but also maximizing your tax savings while proactively getting ahead of tax strategies before it is too late in the year to take advantage of them.

This brings me to your first lessons when it comes to working with accountants. Their primary function in your business is to accomplish two things:

1. Tax preparation—The process of filing your taxes accurately and on time
2. Tax planning—Proactively assessing the individual tax strategies for your business and personal finances that will help you legally save money on your tax bill

I could add an unofficial third function, which is to answer all your questions about taxes as they come up during the year, but those questions will be related to your tax preparation or your tax planning anyway, so we'll keep the functions to a nice, easy two.

While these two functions, tax preparation and tax planning, may seem fairly straightforward, most accountants only offer the tax preparation piece. As they file your taxes, they might suggest some tax savings strategies for the following year, but we can hardly call this tax planning. Their goal is to knock out your personal and business tax returns, and then avoid talking to you until the next tax year. Tax preparation is undoubtedly the most important part of an accountant's service because it keeps the IRS from handcuffing you outside of your home and taking you to jail for tax evasion. However, if your online business is how you make your full-time living, I hope that you aspire for your accountant to do more for you than just keep you out of prison.

I acknowledge that I am painting a bit of a grim picture of accountants here. Of course there are some great accountants out there, but the business model of accounting, at least in America, is primarily a commoditized service. This is why so many accountants simply try to file as many tax returns as they can, at way too low of a price, and then go on vacation for four months once the tax season is over. The pay can be good, but the work-life balance sucks badly for a good three to four months of the year. You would be shocked to hear how toxic the company culture is at many accounting firms because of this.

At the end of the day, you need a tax professional to help you file your taxes as a business owner. Some countries have really straightforward tax systems that do not require the need for their citizens to hire professional help, but in good old America, our tax system is a twisted mess of ambiguity and loopholes. Hiring an experienced accountant to ensure the taxes for your business and personal finances are done properly each year is, in my opinion, nonnegotiable. Doing it yourself, or letting a business partner, relative, friend, or stranger in an alley convince you they can handle it for free, is a recipe for disaster. I have seen the results of free tax preparation firsthand and it is not pretty.

Who Should Be Your Accountant?

In the United States, bookkeepers do not need any formal training or certifications to do bookkeeping. Tax preparation is a different story. There are essentially four different types of tax credentials an accountant can have. They can be a certified public accountant (CPA), an enrolled agent (EA), a tax attorney, or a noncredentialed tax preparer. Please note that in countries other than the United States, the credentials an accountant must receive to file taxes will be different, so please do some research to make sure your accountant is in fact qualified to file your taxes.

At the end of the day, I do not believe the type of credentials your accountant has matters all that much. What matters is that they have some sort of tax credential, are experienced at filing taxes, have good systems and processes, and are willing to answer tax questions in a professional and friendly matter.

> *NOTE TO NON-AMERICAN READERS: If your business does not operate in the United States, you can skip this section and go to the next section about what to expect from your accountant. Please do your own research if you would like to learn more about the types of accountants you can work with in your own country.*

> *NOTE TO AMERICAN READERS: These are very brief descriptions of the various types of accountants you can choose from in the United States. I encourage you to do more research on any of these accounting options in more detail if you would like to better understand the full breadth of what their credentials allow them to do for you and your business.*

Certified Public Accountant (CPA)

CPAs are one of the most common types of accountants that small businesses rely on for tax preparation—so much so that CPA is to accountant as Kleenex is to facial tissue.

Becoming a CPA is not easy. Aside from getting a degree in accounting, they also have to pass a strenuous exam to earn their CPA designation in whichever state they want to practice. Their training goes beyond tax preparation and into the realms of financial statement analysis, auditing, payments and collections, as well as financial record maintenance. This expertise and knowledge is great for CPAs working in or with corporations that have sophisticated tax and financial needs. However, it is rare they utilize all of their training when working with small businesses.

While there is cachet to your accountant being a CPA, their designation does not mean they are guaranteed to deliver an awesome tax service and give you great advice. In fact, most of the CPAs I have worked with over the years give very little tax advice unless prompted by their clients. A lot of business owners think they should only work with a CPA, but that is just not true.

Enrolled Agent (EA)

Enrolled agents are the other most common accountant that online business owners work with for tax support. They are certified by the IRS and must complete a series of intensive exams to earn the designation of EA. While CPAs are trained in a variety of different areas of accounting (hence why their education is more robust), enrolled agents are more focused on just tax preparation and tax strategy.

Many EAs earn their designations so they can start their own tax practices, but accounting firms will often hire EAs to support their staff CPAs. If you are working with an EA, though, chances are they are operating as an individual tax preparer, and are not part of a firm.

Tax Attorney

While most tax attorneys do not get their law degrees in order to become tax preparers, there are some that do file taxes for businesses and individuals. Because tax attorneys have to earn a law degree, many of them stay in the realm of law and will represent individuals and businesses when going up against the state or IRS for tax issues. If your accountant is a CPA or an EA, you could let them represent you if you were audited by the IRS, but many business owners prefer working with a tax attorney instead.

Noncredentialed Tax Preparers

Yes, you can have someone with no credentials whatsoever file your taxes on your behalf. No, you should not let your business partner, spouse, uncle, or neighbor file your taxes if they are not credentialed. I do not care that they have filed their own taxes for the past 10 years—filing taxes for business owners is more complex than individual tax returns. If you are serious about your business and serious about not getting screwed over with an unexpected tax bill, then I cannot emphasize enough how much I do not want you to utilize a friend or family member to do your taxes. Go down this road at your own risk.

What to Expect from Your Accountant

I do not know how to say this gently, so I will be blunt: the business model of filing taxes for individuals and businesses is broken. The work of tax accountants is consolidated into a span of three to four months each year. During those months, things get intense. It is not uncommon for accountants to work 80–120 hours per week during tax season. Tax accounting can be a highly lucrative career, but there can also be high personal costs for those that choose this profession.

Why do you need to know this?

Because the intense, deadline-driven nature of tax accounting shapes the culture of the accounting industry. That culture also shapes the way accountants deal with, support, and serve their clients.

I will preface this next paragraph by saying that I have met a number of really pleasant and customer-focused accountants since I got into the world of accounting, but this has been the exception and not the rule. The number of times I, my business partner, and our team at Evolved Finance have had to interact with rude, gruff, patronizing, disorganized, or impatient accountants while supporting our clients is astounding. As I mentioned before, tax season is extraordinarily stressful, so I have sympathy for every accountant we work with, but it is no excuse for unprofessional behavior and poor customer experience.

Like I said before, there are some outstanding accountants out there. You deserve to be working with one of them. You just need to understand what to look for. Here is what you should be aware of when looking to hire your first accountant or replace your existing one.

1. How does their pricing work?

Are they charging you by the hour? If so, what would cause their hours to fluctuate? Do they charge a flat rate for your business and personal tax returns? If you are not clear on how your accountant's billing works, you might find yourself with an unexpectedly large bill.

2. What is included in their services?

This is where a lot of business owners get frustrated. Sure, they want their accountant to file their taxes during tax time, but what happens when they need their accountant the other 10 months of the year when it's not tax time? Will they answer your tax-related questions as they arise? Will they charge you extra for supporting you with these questions?

3. Do they offer tax strategy sessions or just tax preparation?

A lot of business owners think that if they pay for tax preparation services that it also includes tax strategy services as well. This is rarely the case. The process of building out a tax strategy for a business owner, and then helping them to execute that tax strategy, is a very different process from simply filing their taxes. If your business is still relatively small, you likely do not need an accountant that provides a ton of tax strategy, but if your business is generating a healthy profit, then finding an accountant who delivers on the strategy side of your taxes is invaluable.

4. What is their bedside manner like?

Does your accountant respond to your questions in a friendly and helpful way, or do they make you feel dumb for even asking the question to begin with? Are they willing to hop on a call when needed, or do they only communicate via email? Do they respond in a timely manner to your inquiries, or does it take days or weeks to respond? Just because your accountant is good with numbers and taxes does not mean they are good at customer service. If you dread interacting with your current accountant because they are curt, grumpy, or an overall pain to deal with, it might be time to make a change.

5. How do they stay organized?

Running a tax service is all about staying organized. If you get the sense that your accountant is all over the place, that should be concerning. Tax preparation is about attention to detail and organization. Mistakes happen when accountants have bad systems and processes in place and are simply "winging it" on a daily basis. Modern software makes running an accounting firm easier than ever, but you would be shocked how many accountants shy away from utilizing technology to improve their services.

6. Do they proactively check in on your business?

Does your accountant check in with you throughout the year? Do they follow up with you on the tasks they have assigned you to complete? Do they follow through and deliver on the things they say they will do? Do they explain things well the first time or do you have to ask a million questions to get a full answer? Do they give you enough time to complete tasks for them before important deadlines come due? If you answered no to most of the questions, you are not alone, but if your online business is growing and your tax bill is becoming more substantial, a proactive accountant is worth their weight in gold. When you can trust that your accountant and their team have strong follow-up and execution, you can stress a lot less about getting through the tax season each year.

One thing to keep in mind is that most online business owners uplevel the quality of their accountant as their business grows. You might need a bare bones service at a competitive price in your first few years of business. Later on, you can graduate to an accountant that provides higher levels of service and offers more tax planning as your profits get juicier.

INTERNAL FINANCIAL OPERATIONS

Contrary to popular belief, you do not want to outsource all of your online business's financial responsibilities to your bookkeeper and accountant. There are some financial functions that I believe are best kept inside your business for you or your team to handle. These functions and tasks are what we call internal financial operations. While this phrase is far from sexy, it is not as complicated or scary as it sounds.

Your financial operations consist of all the financial tasks that are not related to filing your taxes or bookkeeping. While these tasks are part of your financial operations, they tend to be more administrative in nature and do not demand any deep financial expertise (especially in comparison to bookkeeping and tax preparation). These financial tasks can also demand a deeper expertise of the daily operations of the business, making it inefficient and expensive to outsource the management of these tasks to an external bookkeeper or accountant.

Common internal financial tasks include:

- Issuing refunds to customers and clients
- Sending invoices
- Collecting money from customers with outstanding invoices
- Creating and/or managing a forecast and budget spreadsheet
- Generating sales reports from the business's sales software
- Setting up and running payroll
- Sending payments to independent contractors and affiliate partners

So who should be responsible for the internal financial operations in your online business? It really depends on how large your business is.

Most online business owners have to manage these tasks themselves in the early stages of their businesses. The good news is, depending on their business model and how much money they're making, only a few of the internal financial tasks I listed earlier would be applicable to them. For instance, most of our clients avoid having to send out invoices because they utilize checkout software to collect payment from their customers. So, no matter how large their business becomes, they will never have to deal with invoicing. Score! On the flip side, once an online business in the United States generates enough profit, their accountant usually recommends that they start paying themselves a monthly salary through payroll (this is part of a common tax strategy in the States). These lucky online business owners now get to add running payroll each month as part of their financial operations going forward. Hooray!

If your online business is generating enough revenue to afford a virtual assistant, operations manager, business manager, or a customer service specialist, then many of these financial tasks would fall onto their plates.

For instance, your customer service person can be responsible for issuing refunds to customers and following up with clients who are late on their payments. Your administrative and operations team members can send out invoices, pay vendors and contractors, manage a forecast and budget spreadsheet, handle your payroll software, and pull sales data from your checkout software. In all of these instances, paying your internal team will almost always be less expensive than paying an outside financial pro like a bookkeeper or an accountant. Plus, all of the important knowledge related to managing these financial tasks stays inside your company, making it easier to train new team members on your financial systems.

Are there some bookkeepers and accountants that manage these tasks for their clients? Yes. Should you want them to manage these financial tasks for your online business? No. It is borderline impossible to be a really good bookkeeper or a really good accountant while also managing all of the other financial tasks for multiple businesses (spoiler alert: you are not their only client). You want your bookkeeper to be as skilled as possible at organizing and reconciling your financial data. If they are also having to manage a bunch of your business's other financial processes, I question how good of a job they are doing with the bookkeeping. The same goes for your accountant. Filing your taxes properly and saving you money on taxes should be their sole focus. Having them do anything outside of these two areas of expertise means they are not putting their full attention into being the best tax strategist and tax preparer they can be.

Here is another way of thinking about this. Would you want your family doctor to also specialize in dentistry and optometry? I sure as hell would not. Being a general practitioner is difficult enough as it is. How could they possibly be a good dentist and a good eye doctor on top of that? It might be convenient to have these three services coming from one doctor, but you sacrifice the quality of those three services by getting them from one person. The same goes for your bookkeeper and accountant.

The last thing I will say here is that, as your business grows, things like payroll, budgeting, accounts payable (paying bills and vendors), and issuing refunds will never go away. The sooner you can build the competency to manage these internal financial tasks within your business, the smoother your operations will be and the more money you will save in the long run. It is truly a win-win.

• ACTION ITEMS •

This chapter has a lot to digest. You do not have to absorb it all in one go-around though. Below are the main components to take away from this chapter.

- If the way the financial side of your business works is still a little hazy, read the first two sections of this chapter again. The more you can understand the basic flow of money through your business, as well as the main financial functions of your business, the more confident you will feel that you are not missing any large financial concepts as your business grows.

- If you know the bookkeeping in your business needs improvement, start looking for your first bookkeeper or a new bookkeeper. Reread the section of this chapter about bookkeeping and use it to help you find a bookkeeper that better serves your business. Especially if your current bookkeeper is you!

- If you are not ready to hire a bookkeeper yet, go to evolvedfinance .com to check out our premade bookkeeping spreadsheet. If you already have your own version of a bookkeeping spreadsheet, then continue using it until the amount of transactions in your business grows to the point that it becomes necessary to move to bookkeeping software and hire a bookkeeper.

- If you are not currently working with an accountant, read the section about accountants again and start your search. If you need to work with a low-cost accountant, do not stress too much about finding someone with all the qualities I laid out in this chapter. If you can afford to work with a more qualified accountant, then use this chapter as a guide to help you find an accountant that can best serve you and your business.

- If you are currently working with an accountant, but this chapter made you realize that you might not be getting the customer experience you want and deserve, then start your search for a new accountant well before tax season begins.

- If you want to get clearer about the internal financial functions in your business, make a list of all the tasks that need to be completed each day, week, or month. Next to each financial task, add the name of the person who is responsible for completing that task. Even if you are responsible for doing all of these tasks now, you can off-load these tasks to other team members as your business grows.

6

Creating a Clean Financial Foundation

During my time working for adidas America, I was introduced to the concept of lean manufacturing, which essentially entails minimizing the waste associated with any operational process in a company. In essence, it means achieving a desired result with as few steps as possible. Toyota invented the idea, and the manufacturing and engineering of their vehicles has been the gold standard in the automotive industry for decades because of how reliable their vehicles are on the road. Toyota accomplishes this by not overengineering their vehicles. The fewer moving parts engineered into a car means there are fewer things to break, making it easier to repair their vehicles when something does break down. This is why Toyota cars and trucks maintain such high prices on the used market and why people are willing to spend thousands of dollars on used Toyotas with 100,000 miles or more on the odometer. This high level of build quality has been a cornerstone of Toyota's success.

No, this is not a paid ad placement for Toyota. I do not even own a Toyota. I also understand that most of you reading this book do not manufacture a physical product. So why bring up lean manufacturing?

So much of running a profitable online business is about keeping things simple—not adding more parts and pieces to your business than necessary to accomplish a goal or complete a task. Complexity is your enemy as an online business owner. It makes every aspect of your business more difficult to manage. The more moving parts, the more opportunity for those parts to break. Fixing those parts can get expensive as well as make your life far more stressful than it needs to be.

The financial side of your business is as susceptible to complexity as any other part of your business. The larger a business becomes, the more complex the finance stuff becomes. There are more transactions to track, more accounts to reconcile, more sales reports to run, and more bills that need to be paid. This is simply a reality of growth, but if you can build a simple, clean, and streamlined financial foundation for your business now, any extra financial complexity that results from your business growing will be so much easier to manage for both you and your team later on down the road. If your financial foundation is a hot mess, it will only get hotter and messier as your business grows. That sounds disgusting. Let's avoid any hot messes if we can.

This chapter is going to teach you how to clean up your financial foundation so you can build a more profitable and efficient business. The more you take what you learn in this chapter and put it into action, the more you will maximize the value of what you will learn in the subsequent chapters of this book. Your bookkeeper and accountant may want to tenderly hold your face in their hands and beam at you with gratitude after you build your improved financial foundation, so be forewarned.

• • • • • •

I want to start out by reminding you that you should not feel ashamed if your online business's finances have become a bit messy. Until the previous chapter, you may not have really understood how money flows through your business. That is very common. You might have also received bad advice from an accountant, bookkeeper, business coach, or business book. This is also very common.

Whatever the state of your financial foundation, and regardless of how long you have been in business, this is your chance to do a reset. I can assure you this will be a worthwhile endeavor. Your future self will thank you.

There are three components to a simple and clean financial foundation.

1. Separate your personal finances from your business's finances.
2. Open the least number of financial accounts possible.
3. Utilize your financial accounts properly when spending or receiving money.

That's it. Seems pretty simple, right? Well, it is—in theory. The execution can be cumbersome. If your business is brand new and you are using this book as your guide to setting it up, then you are saving yourself from a lot of headaches down the road. For those of you who are already in business and making money, the steps I am going to take you through will feel a little more annoying. It will totally be worth it, though. I pinky promise.

STEP 1—SEPARATE YOUR PERSONAL FINANCES FROM YOUR BUSINESS FINANCES

If you already have separate bank accounts for your business and personal finances, and you are crystal clear about why having those is important, then you can skip this section. For everyone else, keep reading.

When you first started your online business, you had no idea if it would make any money. While I know some of you quit your jobs and spent your life savings on investing in your business right from the start, many of us took baby steps toward our commitment to our businesses. That is why most online entrepreneurs use their personal checking accounts for business income and expenses when they first start. To go through the pain of having to open a bank account for a business that you are not even sure is going to make money can feel unnecessary.

I actually do not disagree with this logic. Using your personal bank account for business transactions in the very beginning makes sense for a lot of entrepreneurs who are testing out the waters and are not fully convinced their business is viable. I would even go so far as to say this would be a prudent course of action.

However, there comes a point where the separation of your personal finances and business's finances is no longer optional. If you are so committed to your business that you are reading this book, then the time has probably come for you to start this separation. This is especially true if you are already making a part- or full-time income from your business. That said, even if your business is not generating any revenue and is only spending money on business expenses, it is still a good idea to remove your business from your personal finances (especially given it does not cost you anything but time to do so).

The financial accounts that entrepreneurs normally mix personal and business transactions in are checking accounts and credit cards. Opening a checking account, and potentially a credit card, that you only use for business transactions is one of the easiest ways to gain financial separation between your personal finances and those of your online business. More on this shortly.

"But Parker! It is so much easier to have all my money in one place! If I have a separate checking account for my business, now it is not as convenient to access my money when I need it!"

Fair enough, but there are three main reasons why giving up this small amount of convenience is worth it.

1. **Having dedicated business accounts makes it easier for your bookkeeper and accountant to track business transactions.** When you have personal expenses mixed in with your business expenses, it becomes more cumbersome for your accounting team to create accurate financial reports and maximize your tax write-offs. Unless you are willing to go transaction by transaction with your bookkeeper each month to make sure they are only categorizing your business expenses, they are going to make mistakes. They will either put personal expenses on your business books that are not tax deductible, which could potentially trigger a government audit, or they will ignore business expenses that should be tax write-offs, which means you pay more in taxes than you should. Either way, your bookkeeper will be annoyed, your accountant will be annoyed, you will waste your time constantly helping them to decipher your business transactions from personal transactions, and your business's financial reports will be less reliable.

2. **By creating separate business and personal accounts, you will gain added liability protection for your personal assets.** I know this sounds like legal jargon, but this is important jargon to

understand. In most countries, you can form a business entity to protect your personal assets in the unlikely event that your business is sued. In America specifically, the most common entities that I see online business owners create are LLCs (limited liability companies) and S corporations. Once you have a business entity, this allows you to open bank accounts, credit cards, merchant accounts, and loans through your business entity's name instead of your personal name. This is called creating a "corporate veil." If your business and personal assets are mixed together, this leaves an opening for a person suing you to go after your personal assets, essentially negating the corporate veil your LLC or S corporation is trying to create. If your personal and business finances are truly separate, then you make it much harder for someone suing you to be able to go after your personal assets. I am not a lawyer, so please consult with a business attorney to figure out if a business entity makes sense for your business and what you need to do to receive the full liability protection from your chosen entity. This is especially important if you have substantial personal savings, real estate holdings, retirement accounts, or other personal wealth that you want to protect.

3. **Keeping your business and personal finances separate creates healthier boundaries.** Most online entrepreneurs work from home, work at all times of the day, and are the faces of their companies. The lines between their personal lives and their work lives can blur together. One easy way you can make those lines less blurry is to separate your business and personal finances. Once you truly see your business as something separate from yourself, it's more likely you will make more unbiased and grounded financial decisions for your business as it grows. It is

extremely difficult to do this when you look at your bank account and cannot tell where your money starts and your business's money ends. You will feel more like a business professional once you start treating the money in your business as just that—your business's money.

Are you sold yet? Good! So what's next?

If you have a business entity, you should go and create new financial accounts under your business's legal name. If you are not sure how to do this, give your bank a call to ask them which documents you need to provide them so you can open a checking account, savings account, and potentially a credit card under your business entity's name (your bank's business credit card options might suck, so be ready to shop online for a business credit card). Most banks will not want to open your accounts over the phone, so be prepared to go into your local bank branch with the appropriate business entity documentation.

If you do not have a business entity and, for whatever reason, you are not quite ready to create one, then a simple option would be to open a new checking account under your personal name and use it only for business income and expenses. In the United States, you could also create a DBA (doing business as) and open your checking account under that DBA business name. You can also open a credit card under your personal name (or DBA) and only use it for business transactions. If you already have multiple personal credit cards, you can consider simply designating one of them to your business so you do not have to open a new card. My hope would be that your business would grow to the point that it would eventually make sense to form a business entity, so just know you will have to go through this process again when that time comes.

What other financial accounts should you be creating for your business? And how should you use these accounts? I am glad you asked.

The financial accounts I have listed below are by far the most common accounts we see our clients at Evolved Finance utilize. Depending on your business model, you might not need all of these accounts right away, but for our six- and seven-figure clients, it is very rare that they are not utilizing one of each of the accounts below.

Business Checking Account

Your business checking account should be the primary place where all business-related revenue is received. That revenue typically comes in the form of deposits from your merchant provider (e.g., Stripe, PayPal, Square, QuickBooks online invoicing, etc.), wire transfers, and checks. Yes, you could also deposit any cash received from customers into this checking account, but cash deposits and online businesses do not mix. Avoid receiving cash if at all possible.

You can also use your checking account to pay for business expenses. This can happen in a variety of different ways. You can write checks, send wire transfers, and use the debit card associated with your business checking account. You can also pay off your business credit card(s) and fund your PayPal account (if applicable) using your business checking account.

In the early stages of an online business, most business expenses will be paid for from the checking account, but once a business credit card is opened up, I recommend running as many expenses through that credit card as possible. I will explain more about this in a bit.

When it comes to quantity, you only need one business checking account. Yes, only one. I understand there is a popular financial system that tells entrepreneurs to open multiple business checking accounts. This envelope-based financial system recommends that business owners have dedicated checking accounts for income, operating expenses, profit, taxes, and so on. If this type of system works for you, then more power to you. An envelope system is better than having no financial system at all. That said, managing five to eight checking accounts in your online business is not simple, clean, or efficient. It creates unnecessary bookkeeping complexity and is a bandage for poor bookkeeping and financial reporting processes. Again, if an envelope system works for you, then stick with it. Everything you are learning in this book will complement a system like that, but my hope is that, after reading this book, you can gradually transition away from needing to utilize so many checking accounts.

Business Savings Account

A savings account for your business is not mandatory, especially for a smaller business, but as your revenue grows, having a savings account can be handy. You can use it to hold your business savings (we will expand on how much you should save in a later chapter), reserve the money you are saving for paying taxes, or temporarily hold onto money that you do not want to keep in your checking account because you will need it to pay for a large expense at a later date (e.g., affiliate payments or bonuses for team members).

If you are in the fortunate position of having a lot of cash in your business, then a business savings account can actually protect your money in case your bank fails. In the United States, we call this federal deposit insurance, which is managed by the Federal Deposit Insurance Corporation (FDIC). The FDIC insures bank accounts (including checking) holding up to $250,000 in the rare instance of bank failure. If you live outside of the United States, then research what sort of deposit insurance is offered by the banks where you live. As of 2023, the International Association of Deposit Insurers shows 146 different countries as offering some sort of deposit insurance, so there is a good chance that your bank offers deposit insurance. Do some research just to be sure.

In terms of quantity of savings accounts, most online businesses only need one. That said, it is fairly common to see our clients use two savings accounts—one for their taxes and a second for other business savings needs. Savings accounts are easy to reconcile from a bookkeeping standpoint, so having a couple of savings accounts should not add much complexity to your finances.

Credit Card

A business credit card is a great tool for managing cash flow and earning rewards simply for paying for necessary business expenses. As long as you are paying off the full balance of your credit card each month from your business checking account, then there is little to no risk in using a credit card for your business. Be aware that many contractors are not able to accept credit card payments. The same is true of landlords if you have rent as an expense in your business. Payroll cannot be paid with a credit card either. For almost everything else, though, a credit card will likely be accepted.

To get the full benefit from your credit card, it is important that you consider three things:

1. Not all business credit cards offer rewards, especially if your business credit card is through a smaller regional bank or credit union. A credit card with no rewards points can still make managing cash flow easier, but you are leaving money on the table by not using a card with a rewards program.
2. A personal credit card that you are using for business transactions will not reward you as well as a business credit card. Personal credit cards often provide extra reward points for purchases like fuel, groceries, and travel. While these types of expenses can happen in an online business, they are pretty rare. Business

cards will often reward you for common business expenses such as advertising, software, and office supplies. Their rewards also tend to be more robust. If you are spending a decent chunk of change on business expenses each month, opening a business credit card is usually worth the effort.

3. If you are not able to pay off your credit card each month, the points do not matter. Your priority will not be to maximize your rewards points but to pay off your credit card debt so you are no longer incurring interest expenses each month.

When it comes to quantity, you only need one credit card. As long as your business credit card has a large enough credit limit to cover all of your monthly expenses, then you should be good with just one. Also, when it comes to rewards points, one main credit card that collects all your rewards points is more useful than your rewards points being spread across a number of credit cards.

I understand that some of you have used credit cards to fund your business. A slow year or an overly ambitious growth strategy might have put you in this position. It happens. Prioritize paying down your cards with the highest interest rate or the lowest balance (assuming the balance is low enough that you can pay off the card quickly). As you pay off cards, consider closing them until you have one main credit card that you want to utilize each month. If your main credit card has a low credit limit, then keeping a secondary business credit card as a backup is a reasonable plan. Please note that closing a business credit card does not affect your personal credit score in the United States.

One other thing I want to mention about business credit cards: your ability to open one is dependent on your personal credit score, so if you have less than stellar credit, you may need to give yourself some time to improve your score before you are able to open a business credit card.

PayPal

For a lot of online business owners, PayPal is a necessary evil. From a bookkeeping standpoint, PayPal is the most difficult type of financial account to reconcile due to the complex ways money moves through their platform. I have rarely seen another bookkeeper outside of our team at Evolved Finance properly reconcile a PayPal account. That said, PayPal can be a really great financial tool for online business owners. PayPal is unique because you can use their platform as a merchant account to receive money from your customers as well as use the platform to pay for business expenses.

In terms of using PayPal as a merchant account, their platform does connect with a lot of different checkout software. This allows your customers to pay for your products and/or services with their own PayPal accounts during the checkout process. While most of your customers will likely choose to use their credit cards or debit cards, there is always a small percentage of consumers who prefer using PayPal to make purchases online. You can also use PayPal to send payment requests to clients, which can be nice when you need to send an invoice in a pinch. There are far better invoicing platforms out there, but it is convenient that you have the option to do this in PayPal.

There is one type of expense for which it can make sense to use your PayPal account: contractors. Specifically, contractors that are working for your business from other countries. You can also conveniently pay multiple people through PayPal's mass pay feature, which is specifically helpful when there is a need to pay a high volume of affiliate partners at once. Outside of contractors, there is not really a good reason to pay for other business expenses through PayPal. Your business credit card or debit card will do the trick.

You only want one PayPal account for your online business. I cannot emphasize enough how difficult it is to reconcile PayPal accounts from a bookkeeping standpoint. If you have more than one PayPal account, your bookkeeper will likely want to drop you as a client. If they do not drop you, then you can be fairly confident that they are not properly entering the financial data from PayPal into your bookkeeping software.

One last thing. You will want to make sure that you have a business PayPal account. These types of PayPal accounts allow you to take advantage of many of the features I mentioned earlier while also providing better financial reporting.

Merchant Account

A merchant account is a type of business bank account that allows your business to process electronic payments from your customers. Without a merchant account, an online business would not be able to process credit card and debit card payments from their customers through the internet. Stripe is by far the most popular merchant provider in the online space because of how seamlessly their merchant account connects to different checkout software, but I have seen online businesses utilize other merchant providers as well. If your business operates outside of the United States, then you might not have Stripe as a merchant account option.

It is important to know that merchant accounts act differently from PayPal. As I mentioned earlier, PayPal can operate as a merchant account, but it can act as a checking account as well. That means money can sit in your PayPal account until you transfer it to your business bank account. A merchant account like Stripe is different. During a normal transaction, a merchant account will hold your money for two to eight days. They will then remove their fee, which is usually 3–5% of the total sale, and deposit the net amount into your business bank account. Please note that the length of time your merchant provider holds onto your money and the amount of money they charge per transaction will be dependent on which merchant provider you work with.

Outside of PayPal, the goal for any online business is to only utilize one merchant account. Reconciling merchant accounts from a bookkeeping perspective can be very tricky, so having multiple merchant accounts increases the chances that your bookkeeping is done incorrectly. Issuing refunds can also get overly complicated if you and/or your team have to go to multiple merchant accounts to issue refunds to different customers.

Find one merchant account that works with all of your checkout software and you will make massive strides toward building a simple and clean financial foundation.

Sales Software

In quantum mechanics, there is a theory that there are an infinite number of universes. I like to imagine that in one of those universes, every online business only utilizes one sales software for their entire business. Unfortunately, this is not the reality for our universe.

What is sales software?

It is any software platform that allows their users to create a checkout page—the page where you enter your billing info so you can pay for something on the internet. Aside from the ability to create checkout pages, great sales software also allows you to pull sales reports so you can analyze your sales data.

While there are dedicated software platforms for building checkout pages, many of the clients we work with at Evolved Finance utilize the checkout page functionality built into one of the software platforms they are already using. That could be the software they use to host their course or membership site, their customer relationship management (CRM) software, their website platform, or their landing page software.

As a reminder, your merchant account processes the payment from your clients and deposits the money into your business checking account. Your sales software simply creates the checkout page that captures your customer's payment information and then transfers that information to your merchant account for processing. This is why you typically have to connect your merchant account to your checkout software during the setup process. Otherwise, the checkout functionality of your sales software would be useless.

> *Side Note #1: If you are not aware of having opened a merchant account, but you have a checkout page that your customers are using to pay for your products and/or services via credit and debit cards, then your checkout software likely has a merchant account built into its checkout functionality. If this is the case, you are likely paying higher merchant fees than if you simply opened your own merchant account and connected it to your checkout software yourself. I would recommend looking at the merchant fees associated with this type of sales software to see if you could save money by opening your own dedicated merchant account.*

> *Side Note #2: Not all of your revenue needs to flow through your sales software and merchant account. If you receive royalty payments from a sponsor, affiliate payments from an affiliate partner, or any other form of direct payment via wire or check, then please know this is a very common way to receive income into your business.*

Ideally, you are only utilizing one checkout software for your business. Having every sale you make go through one main sales platform is helpful for one essential reason: it is operationally efficient. You and your team only have to log in to one place to track sales and find customer data. This means fewer mistakes when collecting sales data, less time trying to find sales data, and less money spent on multiple sales software products.

For many online businesses, asking them to consolidate their sales software to one main platform is not always an easy ask. If you need to clean up this part of your financial foundation, please know it will not happen overnight, but I encourage you to do some creative problem-solving around this challenge. Sometimes, that means reflecting on if you are selling too many different offers, which, as you will learn later in this book, can be one of the biggest profit killers for an online business.

Loans and Lines of Credit

For many classic businesses, utilizing loans and lines of credit is a must. There is simply no way their businesses can grow and expand without borrowing money to buy more equipment, rent more space, or buy more inventory. This is not the case for most online businesses. As we discussed earlier in the book, online businesses need very little up-front capital, and most online businesses are profitable enough that they can invest in their growth using their own cash flow. All that said, online entrepreneurs are not immune to financial difficulty and sometimes have to borrow money to keep their businesses afloat. We have seen a number of our clients at Evolved Finance resort to taking out business loans or opening up lines of credit in order to deal with cash flow issues.

When it comes to business loans, they tend to have better interest rates than credit cards. That said, there are more lenders than ever offering loans with predatory interest rates to struggling businesses of all sorts. If you need a business loan, explore your options for the best interest rate you can find and only borrow what you absolutely need. We have seen many of our clients dig their way out of debt relatively quickly, but we have also seen online business owners weighed down by loan payments that cripple their growth for many years. Consider all of your options before taking on a business loan of any sort.

Lines of credit (LOCs) are a bit different. They are like having a checking account full of money you can borrow from only when you need it. You are only charged interest on the amount of money you transfer from your LOC, which can be convenient when you only need a small amount of money to get you through a cash crunch during any given week. For some online business owners, knowing they have an LOC at their disposal in case of an emergency can be comforting, but as with any business loan, online business owners should only borrow money as a last resort.

· · · · · ·

To recap, the financial accounts for your online business would ideally look something like this:

1 business checking account
1–2 business savings accounts
1 business credit card
1 merchant account
1 PayPal account (optional)
1 sales software
0 loans or lines of credit

If you have fewer financial accounts than what you see above, then great! Depending on the size and nature of your online business, you may not need to have all of these accounts. If you are on the other side of the coin and have far more financial accounts than what is listed above, then it would be prudent to set aside some time to consolidate. If you asked me to prioritize the accounts you should consolidate first, I would rank them in this order (from highest priority to lowest).

1. **PayPal**—Multiple PayPal accounts is a bookkeeping nightmare. Get down to one account as soon as possible.
2. **Merchant accounts**—Similar to PayPal, extra merchant accounts are a pain for bookkeepers and make your sales operations more complex.
3. **Checking accounts**—At the very least, make one checking account the only place your business receives revenue. Receiving business income in multiple checking accounts can get messy and confusing.
4. **Credit Cards**—Extra credit cards are less of a bookkeeping concern than the financial accounts above, but the sooner you consolidate down to one main business card, the sooner you maximize reward points.
5. **Sales Software**—You may want to prioritize consolidating your sales software if the pain of collecting money from your customers from so many different places is becoming too cumbersome for you and your team to keep track of.
6. **Savings Accounts**—These are the easiest accounts to consolidate and the easiest accounts to reconcile from a bookkeeping standpoint.

Look at your calendar, block off some time, and consolidate those financial accounts!

MANAGING YOUR BUSINESS EXPENSES

Now that you know the types of financial accounts your online business should be utilizing, we need to make sure we know which expenses we should be running through them. Please know that I am only familiar with the American tax code, so if you live outside of the United States, you will want to confirm with your accountant the types of expenses you are allowed to deduct in your home country.

Before we talk about expenses, let's review your income first. All business-related income should be deposited into your business checking account. Common deposits would be:

- Merchant deposits (e.g., Stripe)
- Checks
- Wire transfers
- Transfers from your business PayPal account
- ACH transfers

You *do not* want to include any paychecks from an employer, birthday checks from your grandma, or reimbursements from your friend for dinner. These are examples of personal income and should be deposited into your personal checking account.

Income is easy. Expenses can be a bit murkier. At least in America, the tax code is not always black and white. There can be nuance around what constitutes a business expense, especially when so many online businesses blur the lines between business and personal life. This is where a good accountant can help you decide on those borderline expenses. For the sake of this book, though, I am going to stick to the more obvious expenses and let you work with your accountant on the expenses that are not so clear. Consider this list of expenses as a foundation you can build on as your business grows and your list of business expenses gets more diverse.

As a reminder, if you have a business credit card, you want to use it to pay for as many of the expenses in your business as you can. For everything else, you can use your checking account and, as a last resort, your business PayPal account (especially for paying contractors and affiliates).

Here is a list of the most common expenses we see in online businesses:

- Advertising expenses
- Affiliate payments
- Bank fees
- Business insurance
- Business travel expenses
- Continuing education (business coaches, courses, seminars, books, etc.)
- Employee payroll
- Hardware expenses (computer, podcast equipment, webcam, etc.)
- Independent contractors (web design, copywriting, virtual assistant, etc.)
- Legal and other professional fees (accountant, bookkeeper, lawyer, etc.)
- Live event expenses
- Marketing expenses
- Meals
- Merchant fees
- Office supplies
- Office utilities
- Rent
- Software expenses
- Website expenses

Depending on your business model and how much revenue your business is generating, there are many more expenses you can likely run through your business, but this is a good starting place for anyone new to entrepreneurship. If you are working with an accountant and/or bookkeeper, they will be able to help you figure out any other expenses you should be running through your business.

One thing to keep in mind is if your accountant and/or bookkeeper is not familiar with online businesses, you might need to be ready to justify some of your expenses. Let me share an example.

We had a client who built a large YouTube following around fashion and style. Her content was based around buying clothes and showing people how to create different looks with the pieces she purchased. This meant she spent a significant amount of money on clothing each year that was the focus of her content, and subsequently, central to her business model.

In the United States, the tax code is very clear about clothing. Unless the clothes are for a professional uniform (medical, construction, security, etc.), a business owner cannot run their wardrobe expenses though their business. Have we had clients try to do this in the past? Yes. Do their accountants let them do this? No.

Our client with the YouTube channel was a different story. She was not buying clothes simply because she wanted to look nice for an event or meeting. She was spending money on the production of her videos, which is a legitimate business expense. This is why her accountant was comfortable writing off the purchases when tax time came around. If her accountant did not understand her business model, they may have removed her clothing expenses from the books, which would have lost her thousands of dollars a year in tax savings.

So I will say this one last time. If you feel that you have legitimate expenses for your online business that are atypical when compared to other business models, be prepared to explain your case to your accountant and bookkeeper. You might not always be correct in your assertion (your accountant is the tax expert, after all), but the times your accountant does agree with you could save you thousands of dollars a year in taxes.

• ACTION ITEMS •

Cleaning up the financial foundation of your online business is like cleaning your home. It is not difficult for an able-bodied person to vacuum floors, wipe down surfaces, and put away clutter. It just sucks because most of us find it boring and time-consuming. There are so many other things we would rather do with our time. I understand that the action items below might feel the same, but the difference between these tasks and cleaning your house is that cleaning your toilet does not have the potential to save you money on taxes, make your business more profitable, or streamline your operations for growth.

Here is a recap of the action items from this chapter.

- If you haven't done so yet, create dedicated financial accounts for your business.
- If you have a business entity, make sure your financial accounts are set up under the name of your business.
- After you have set up your business's financial accounts, make sure you move all business income and all business expenses into and out of those accounts.
- If you have too many financial accounts for your business, see how you can consolidate them to just the accounts listed in this chapter. Some consolidation is better than no consolidation at all.
- Get on the same page with your bookkeeper and accountant about the nature of your online business. The more they understand your business model, the more helpful they can be when it comes to deciding what types of expenses you can write off as tax deductions.

PART 3

The Four Profit Pillars

This is where the rubber meets the road. Everything you have learned in parts one and two of this book has been to prepare you to meet the four profit pillars. The next four chapters will teach you how to set up, analyze, problem-solve, and pay yourself through the lens of the Profit Pillars system.

7

The Goal of the Profit Pillars System . . . Generate a Profit!

Since 2014, I've looked at thousands of financial statements for all types of online businesses. I've met hundreds of online entrepreneurs, many of whom I now call friends and colleagues, and have seen their businesses blossom in front of my eyes. Some of these entrepreneurs are experienced business professionals with degrees and past careers that helped them to get where they are. Others are passionate creatives and dreamers who did the work to figure out how the world of business works, despite not having much business experience. Regardless of the entrepreneur's background or past experiences, one of the universal truths I have uncovered after seeing behind the scenes of so many successful online businesses is that a *profitable* business rarely happens by accident.

Let me repeat that one more time.

A profitable business rarely happens by accident.

Have we worked with clients who fell into their businesses without really planning on becoming entrepreneurs? Yup. Have we seen entrepreneurs have some luck with their marketing strategies and suddenly see their revenue double, triple, or even quadruple in a year? We sure have. Have we seen clients nonchalantly generate huge profits year over year without paying attention to their numbers? Nope. There are plenty of ways entrepreneurs can benefit from luck or good fortune, but it just does not happen when it comes to profit.

I have seen clients have tremendously successful years during which their revenue grows so fast they can barely keep up, allowing them to have a six-to-twelve-month period when their business is very profitable without putting any intention into actually being profitable. Unfortunately, it is only a matter of time before they overcompensate for their rapid revenue growth by increasing their expenses too quickly, which ends with bank balances that can be very stressful to look at.

Keeping your business profitable as it grows takes intention and visibility into your numbers. It means learning to play Game #2 (managing your business's cash flow). I do not care how heart-centered your business is or how much of a marketing genius you are, if you do not learn how to generate a profit, your business is going to feel like it is all hustle and stress but without a payoff.

WHY IS PROFIT SO IMPORTANT FOR ONLINE BUSINESSES?

I know this question sounds basic but hang with me for just a moment.

Not every business model relies on turning a big profit in order to build the wealth of the business owner. In the world of tech start-ups, there have been a number of founders who became overnight millionaires (or sometimes even billionaires) after selling their business to a larger company, despite the business not being profitable. There have also been numerous start-ups that have gone public (also known as an IPO) despite their companies having never turned a profit. These founders also became millionaires and billionaires despite the poor financial state of their companies.

These types of businesses are focused on building the value of the company, and as you just learned, value does not always coincide with profitability. Value might reside in capturing early market share from competing start-ups or developing patents for innovative new technologies. When this is the case, the founders of start-ups like these can worry about profitability later. As long as investors and shareholders perceive the company as being more valuable in the future, they will keep investing money into the start-up until the company is purchased, goes public, or goes bankrupt (not the preferred result).

This is a very different game from the one you are playing as an online business owner. While it is not fair to say online businesses are worthless, it is true that the overwhelming majority of online businesses would never be able to find a potential buyer. Even if they did, the purchase price would hardly be life changing.

Does this mean you should close down your online business and get into the world of tech start-ups? Of course not. For every tech start-up that has a gazillion-dollar IPO or is acquired by Google for a bajillion dollars, there are thousands of other start-up companies that have failed. Many of these founders made little to no income while their business was in early start-up phases and many of them even dumped their life savings into keeping the business afloat. Start-ups are extremely high risk and high reward. Start-up founders love the high reward part to the point that they can easily forget about the risk.

Online businesses are not nearly as risky as tech start-ups. There are a few reasons for this.

- The up-front costs to start an online business are minimal. In fact, many online business owners do not spend a dime until after they land their first client or customer. The barrier to entry is almost nonexistent.
- Online businesses can be successful with a modest customer base. Most start-ups need thousands of customers to even have a chance at turning a profit.
- Online businesses can operate with very low overhead expenses, which means they have the potential for extraordinarily high profit margins.

That last bullet point brings us full circle.

Online businesses have the potential for profit unlike any other business model I have seen. All they need is an online presence, some savvy marketing tactics, and a digital offer or service that can be sold on the internet to customers all over the world (or, at the very least, all over their country of residence). This is the recipe for a business model where expenses can remain low relative to the amount of revenue that can be generated.

Think of it this way. If you wanted to open a restaurant in your town, your customer base would be limited to the people living in a 10- to 15-mile radius around your location. On top of that, you would likely need to take out a loan to cover the high start-up costs involved with getting your restaurant off the ground. Expenses like the lease for your space, the initial inventory of ingredients used to cook the dishes, various equipment and supplies, decor, and the hiring costs for employees who will cook and serve the food. These expenses do not go away once the restaurant opens its door either. Most of these expenses reoccur every month, meaning you have to bring in enough revenue to not just cover your monthly overhead costs, but to also pay back the initial start-up loan. Is it any wonder that new restaurants fail at such a high rate?

An online business can get their first customer with nothing more than a social media profile. That customer could also live in another state or even another country. An online business does not have to deal with exorbitant start-up costs, is not limited to finding customers in their local area, and can keep their overhead costs extremely low until they are ready to scale. This is such an advantage from a business model standpoint that I wish I could type the last couple of paragraphs in all caps to emphasize how bonkers this is (my editor made the correct decision to not let me do that).

The sooner you can internalize the fact that your business is not a tech start-up with an IPO in its future, nor is there a giant corporation waiting to offer you millions of dollars for your online business, the sooner you can prioritize tracking and maximizing your profitability. This is the advantage your online business has over almost every other business model in existence. Take advantage of it. Profit is your tool for building wealth.

I would know better than most. I have watched hundreds of online businesses have astoundingly profitable years. They do not have to wait for someone to purchase their business to build their wealth. They make their money now. There is nothing tricky about it. They run profitable businesses and pay themselves from that profit. For many of our clients, their online businesses pay them an above average salary that far surpasses anything they would have made in their previous careers. For other clients, they amass wealth that is normally reserved for doctors, lawyers, and C-suite executives.

Building a profitable online business provides more benefits than just paying your salary though. Through your business's profits, you can:

- Build cash reserves so a single month of poor sales does not mean forgoing your salary, taking on high interest debt, or pulling money from your personal savings.

- Invest back into your business in bigger ways without having to take out loans or max out credit cards.

- Donate to charitable causes and make a bigger impact in the world.

- Make strategic business decisions from a calm and secure place because you are not dealing with the pressure that comes from being in a challenging cash flow situation.

- More easily set yourself up to qualify for personal car loans and mortgages by showing lenders that your business is financially solvent and a reliable source of income for your household. This is especially important if you are the breadwinner of your family.

Everything about operating your business is easier when its profit margins are in a great place, but this is easier said than done. Yes, online businesses have the potential for higher profit margins than most other business models, but you still have to make an effort to take advantage of the profit potential in your business. You cannot just assume it will happen automatically.

HOW PROFITABLE SHOULD MY
ONLINE BUSINESS BE?

Before I answer this question, we should do a quick overview of how to track profitability in your business. While we have covered some of the details about this topic already, I want to put all the pieces together for you.

Tracking the profitability of your online business starts with your bookkeeper. As we discussed in an earlier chapter, your bookkeeper categorizes and reconciles all of the financial transactions in your business. The purpose of doing so is to make it easy to generate financial reports. The most important financial report for any online business owner to review each month is their profit and loss statement. As the name suggests, this report is the key to keeping track of your monthly, quarterly, and yearly profits.

The math behind a profit and loss statement is very simple.

Revenue

- Expenses

Profit

We will explore what makes up the expenses in an online business in greater detail in chapter eight, but for now, this basic formula is the key to monitoring the most important metric in your online business: your profitability.

So how profitable should your online business be?

At Evolved Finance, we want our clients to strive for at least a 30% profit margin. That means for every $1,000 of revenue generated, at least $300 should be staying in the business as profit.

For online businesses offering services, we lower the profit expectations to 20%. This is because service-based businesses have much higher labor costs than online businesses selling digital products. While online service businesses have a lower profit ceiling than other online businesses, they do tend to be more valuable if the owner wants to sell the business down the road.

So how did I come to the 30% conclusion? By analyzing our clients' profit and loss statements each year since 2010. Between myself and our team at Evolved Finance, we have looked at tens of thousands of profit and loss statements during this time period. Through all this analysis, the patterns became clear. A profit margin of 30% or better was consistently achievable for online businesses.

When I first partnered with Corey back in 2014, we were recommending profit margins of 40% to our clients. This was the trend until around 2018–2019. At that point, increased competition in the online business space in combination with the increased costs associated with running an online business meant we no longer believed every online business had the potential to turn a profit of 40%. Hence, we now urge our clients to push for a 30% margin at a minimum.

To give you an idea of how amazing a 30% profit margin is, here is how other industries compare.

- Brick-and-mortar retail businesses have an average net profit of 10%.
- Manufacturing businesses have an average net profit of 5–10%.
- Restaurants have an average net profit of 5–10%.

Now before you run off and cut every expense in your online business so you can get your profitability to 30% or better, I want to share some more context around profitability for online businesses.

Profitability Is Not the Goal in the Beginning

Smaller online businesses are not able to prioritize profit in the early stages of their development. For instance, if your business averages $1,000 per month in revenue with an average of $900 per month in expenses, that leaves you with $100 per month of profit (10% profit margin). Cutting back on expenses to improve profitability is likely not the best course of action in this case. Most of these expenses will be foundational for the future of your business, so focusing on driving more sales should be the priority over cutting your expenses.

Investing in Growth Lowers Your Profit Temporarily

It is an obvious concept, but you have to invest in your online business for it to grow. That investment could be a website redesign, hiring a new key team member, or working with an experienced consultant or coach. Either way, you likely will not get an immediate return on these types of investments. That means taking a temporary hit in profit now so you can make a larger profit later on. If I could tell you what investments to make in your online business that would guarantee a return, then this book would sell 100 million copies. While I am not able to tell you what to invest in, I can tell you that the years when you make larger investments in your online business might mean having a lower profit margin than the previous year. That is okay. As long as you are comfortable with giving up the profit now to fulfill your vision of a more successful business down the road, then a dip in profit is nothing to be ashamed of.

How Much You Work Impacts Profitability

This might be the biggest bummer in the entire book, but do not kill the messenger. From my many years monitoring the financial status of all kinds of different online businesses, I have found that the less the owner of an online business works, the less profit the business generates. Why? Because whatever work the business owner is not doing needs to be done by someone else. That usually means taking on more labor costs (contractors and/or employees) to cover the work that the owner is not doing themselves.

Please understand that there is nothing wrong with this strategy. Sometimes online business owners want to spend more time with family, take a mental health break, or are simply okay with making less money but having more leisure time. All of these are acceptable reasons to work less. As long as you can accept the possibility of your profit margin shrinking, there is nothing wrong with giving up earning potential for a business that can run without your daily involvement.

Profit Is Not the Only Way You Are Compensated as a Business Owner

Profitability does not always represent the full financial benefit the business owner is receiving from their company. Let's say your online business has a profit margin of 20%. That means 80% of your business's revenue is going to business expenses. While 80% is a significant amount of your business's revenue, not all business expenses are created equal. Some of these expenses might benefit you directly, such as paying a portion of your personal rent, your monthly payroll salary, your company retirement plan, or your personal utilities. If you add these types of expenses back into your profit, the benefit you are receiving as the owner starts to look much better than just the 20% profit margin showing up at the bottom of your profit and loss statement.

If you look at the example on the next page, you will notice that this business generated $500,000 in revenue, had $350,000 in total expenses, and was left with a profit of $150,000. While the 30% profit margin is great, it does not tell the full story.

Revenue	$500,000
Owner Payroll	$100,000
Rent & Utilities	$15,000
Other Expenses	$235,000
Total Expenses	$350,000
Profit	$150,000
	30% Profit

If you break down the $350,000 in total expenses into greater detail, you will see that the owner of the business was paid a payroll salary of $100,000 for the year. They were also able to write off $15,000 in utilities and rent for their home office. This is $115,000 worth of expenses that are directly benefiting the owner. That equates to 23% of the total revenue. If we add those owner benefits to the 30% profit margin, that is 53% of the total revenue benefiting the owner. That is over half of the revenue generated!

All of this is to say, your profit margin does not tell you the entire story of how your business benefits you as the owner. Taking into consideration the owner benefit expenses hiding in your business can make a huge impact on how stressed you feel when looking at your profit and loss statement each month.

You Can Do Better Than 30%

A 30% profit margin is not the pinnacle of profitability for online businesses. We have seen many of our clients at Evolved Finance achieve much higher profit margins than this. In fact, when I joined Evolved

Finance in 2014 and started seeing our clients' profit and loss statements, I could not believe how profitable some of these businesses were.

For instance, it is not uncommon for our clients to achieve 35–45% profit margins in a given year, regardless of how much revenue they generated. I believe most online businesses can achieve these types of margins, too, but they need to have sound business practices to do so.

We also have clients who can achieve profit margins of 50–70% in a given year. This is less common, but still possible. Should you expect these types of profit margins for your own business? Probably not. For instance, my business partner and I would never expect profits like this for Evolved Finance because we are a service-based business with high employee costs, but if we were only selling digital products, these margins might be possible.

How much profit you can generate beyond the 30% benchmark depends on a number of factors. Not all of these factors are within your control (including luck), but if you effectively manage the ones that you can control, a profit margin of at least 30% (20% for online service businesses) should be achievable for any online business.

HOW DO YOU MAKE YOUR ONLINE BUSINESS MORE PROFITABLE?

During my time as a US product manager for adidas America, I had the pleasure of working with a regional sales manager who had a brilliant way of using simple concepts to get his team motivated and focused. We can call him Bob. Bob coined a phrase during a meeting I attended that went viral in our office and it still sticks with me today. That phrase is "sell more shit." Yes, it is a bit simplistic and crass, but during the meeting in which he uttered those genius words, it was exactly what the team needed to hear. We all laughed when he said it, but in that moment, it helped everyone in the room get focused on what really mattered. We were a manufacturing company that sold physical products to retailers. There was never a time where we did not need to be "selling more shit." It is amazing how easy it is to forget this simple fact.

That leads me to the first way you can make your business more profitable: sell more shit.

Easier said than done, but for so many online businesses, expenses are not the issue. Their lack of sales is the problem. Every business needs to drive revenue for their business model to work, and this issue is especially obvious for newer or smaller online businesses who are struggling to make enough money to create a full-time income for themselves. Yes, they can still have expenses that are too high, but cash flow becomes a lot easier to manage when sales are coming in.

If you read chapter three, you also know that generating more sales is not the only answer for solving profitability issues in your business, especially if your business is making six or seven figures in revenue each year. In this case, cutting business expenses can make sense, as long as the expenses you cut do not significantly reduce the business's revenue. For instance, if your business relies on promoting to an email list in order to drive revenue, it would be destructive to cancel your email marketing software to save money. On the flip side, if your business is spending thousands of dollars a year on software that you and your team barely even use, then it would probably be a good idea to cancel those software subscriptions.

If you really want to see your business get more profitable, you can pull a double whammy and increase revenue while cutting back on unnecessary expenses. This might seem like a pipe dream, but I have seen online businesses do this. Especially if they have been growing a lot and are gaining financial insight into their business for the first time. That is when they can find opportunities to streamline their expenses without sacrificing their continued revenue growth.

So, to recap, you have three options when it comes to generating more profit in your business:

1. Increase your revenue while keeping expenses the same.
2. Keep your revenue the same but decrease your expenses.
3. Increase your revenue while decreasing your expenses (double whammy!).

For some of you reading this, you might be saying, "No duh!" I understand the math is simple here, but so many entrepreneurs get so wrapped up in the details of their businesses that they can forget the simple nature of what they are trying to achieve. Sell more than you spend. Simplifying what you are trying to accomplish financially with your online business can spur the creativity needed to find solutions that will hopefully move your profitability in the right direction.

As simple as all this sounds, to know what sort of action you need to take in your online business to improve its profitability takes financial visibility. You cannot simply look at your credit card statement or your bank balance and suddenly have the insights you need to make impactful financial changes. This is why your bookkeeping is so important. If your bookkeeper organizes your financial transactions in a way that makes it easier to see where you can make financial improvements in your business, you can spend less time trying to figure out what's wrong in your business and more time fixing issues and taking advantage of financial opportunities.

Luckily, you are going to learn in the next chapter how you can start organizing the expenses in your business so you can more easily assess its financial health.

The Four Profit Pillars of Your Online Business

Profit is one of the easiest financial metrics to calculate in your online business. Subtract your total expenses from your total revenue and what's left over is profit. But if profit is such an easy concept, why do so many online businesses struggle with it? Why do they not know how much profit their online business is generating? Why are they not clear on the biggest factors affecting their profitability?

The most common reasons I have seen for online businesses not being more in touch with their profits are:

- They lack financial reporting because they do not have a bookkeeper.
- Their bookkeeper waits to do all the categorization and reconciling at the end of the year, making it too late to act on any financial insights gained from reviewing their numbers.

- Their bookkeeping is done so poorly that they cannot trust the accuracy of the financial data that is presented to them.
- Their bookkeeper is organizing their financial data in such a way that it does not make sense to the business owner.
- The business owner is ignoring the financial data being presented to them.

Aside from the last point, the common denominator here is bookkeeping. If nobody is tracking the financial transactions in your business, you will not have any financial reporting. If you do not have any financial reporting or the reports you receive are inaccurate or overly confusing, then you will be in the dark about how to make strategic changes in your business to help it become more profitable.

The way your bookkeeper organizes your profit and loss statement can vary tremendously. The most common issues we have seen are:

- The bookkeeper uses only a handful of very broad expense categories that leaves the business owner with zero insights into the details of what the business is spending money on.
- The bookkeeper uses too many expense categories, making the profit and loss statement look messy and overwhelming. This level of excessive detail leaves no room for the business owner to see the macro-level trends of their finances.
- The bookkeeper uses expense categories that are found on government tax forms or are used in unrelated industries, leaving the business owner confused about how those expense categories are applicable to their online business model.

Evolved Finance has developed a system for organizing the expenses in an online business so that it is easy for our clients to catch profitability issues without the need for a high-priced CFO or financial consultant.

The core of this system is what I call the four profit pillars. Each pillar consists of a collection of expenses that make up the four most important functions of your online business. If you manage each of these pillars effectively, you will have a profitable online business.

The four profit pillars of an online business are:

1. **Lead and Conversion Expenses**—These are all of the direct costs associated with converting your leads into customers.
2. **Offer Delivery Expenses**—These are all of the direct costs associated with delivering your digital product(s) or service(s) to your customers.
3. **Labor Expenses**—This is the total cost of the contractors and/or employees that support your business.
4. **Operations Expenses**—This is the total cost of all the other more general operating expenses in the business.

Think of these four profit pillars as the main buckets that hold all of the expenses that occur in your online business. These pillars consist of other, smaller expense categories (which we will review shortly) that when grouped together offer deep financial insights that actually help you find profitability issues quickly and easily. Large companies have the benefit of employing a CFO and a team of analysts and accountants to pore over all of the financial data every day. Small businesses do not have this luxury. By utilizing the Profit Pillars system, you get CFO-level insights without the need for a large finance team.

We have been using the four profit pillars across hundreds of different online businesses and the results have been astonishing. After one call with our team to review the metrics around their four profit pillars, the business owner is able to understand how money is moving in and out of their business like never before. There are two reasons for this. The first one is that it's simple. Monitoring four expense buckets is much easier than monitoring dozens of individual expenses on your profit and loss statement each month. Our clients still look at those individual expense categories on their profit and loss statements, but their profit pillars help them understand which of the smaller expense categories need their attention.

The second reason the four profit pillars are so helpful is because they represent a more logical way of thinking about how money moves through a business. Most profit and loss statements are a bunch of expense categories stacked on top of each other with little rhyme or reason. This way of presenting financial data does not help the business owner understand the story of how money is moving through their business. By grouping the expense categories on your profit and loss statement together in a more strategic manner, your ability to gather insights from your numbers increases dramatically. The image below offers a visual representation of what I mean by this.

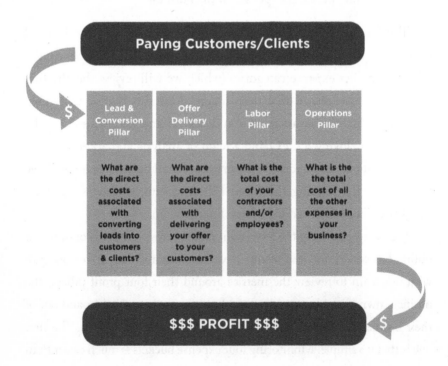

There is one caveat to the way we group expenses together under the four profit pillars. If you sell any sort of physical products, your bookkeeper and accountant will likely need to utilize an expense category called cost of goods sold (COGS). COGS includes all the expenses related to the production of a product. Manufacturing businesses regularly deal with COGS. E-commerce and retail businesses deal with COGS quite a bit because they typically purchase and hold inventory in their garage, stockroom, or warehouse.

The online businesses we serve at Evolved Finance rarely have COGS because they generate the bulk of their revenue through offers and services with no direct production costs. These revenue streams include services, digital products, royalties, speaking fees, sponsorship fees, book advances, and so on. There are occasions where we do have clients with COGS, but they constitute such a small amount that it has little to no impact on the business's profitability. All of this to say, if you have a small number of physical products that you sell in your online business, your accountant or bookkeeper will need to track the COGS associated with those physical products in their own "expense bucket" outside of the four profit pillars.

· · · · · ·

Now that we have a basic overview of what the four expense pillars are and how they will help you understand the way money moves through your online business, let's dive deeper into the expenses that make up each pillar. Before we do that, though, let's visualize what the four pillars might look like as a profit and loss statement. The following image is a very simplified version of a profit and loss statement. All of the revenue sits at the top, the four profit pillars are subtracted out from that revenue, and what is left over at the bottom is the profit.

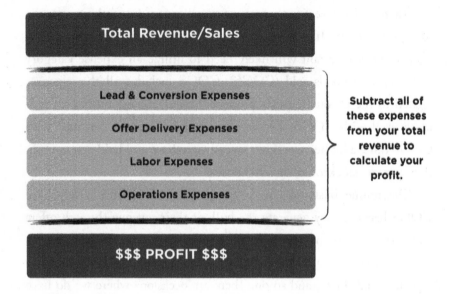

Before we dive into each profit pillar individually, it is important that you understand a financial concept called "percentage of revenue." This is where you look at any expense in your business as a percentage of the revenue your business generates. To make this clearer, let's look at an example.

If your online business was spending $12,000 a year on business software, you wouldn't know if that was a lot of money unless you looked at that $12,000 in the context of your total revenue.

If the yearly revenue for your business was $300,000, then that $12,000 software expense would represent 4% of your total revenue for the year. If your total revenue for the year was only $30,000, then that $12,000 software expense would represent 40% of your revenue. Spending 4% of your revenue on software is not something you are likely going to lose sleep over, but if your software expenses represent 40% of your total revenue, you might consider canceling some of your app subscriptions.

Looking at your expenses as percentages instead of hard numbers can be a game changer. It helps to take the "feel" out of looking at your numbers. It does not matter if $12,000 "feels" like a big or small number to you. It only matters if that $12,000 is taking up a large or small percentage of your revenue. If you are someone who is hesitant to invest in your business to help it grow, percentages can free you up to not be so tightfisted with your business's cash. If you are more of a free spender, percentages can help you realize where you might be going overboard with your expenses and provide you with more accountability.

The goal of monitoring your profit pillars is to help you achieve a profit margin of 30% or better (20% or better for agencies and service-based online businesses). If you need a refresh on profitability, reread chapter seven.

Now for the fun part. Let's learn more about each of the four profit pillars of an online business.

LEAD AND CONVERSION PILLAR

The lead and conversion pillar consists of all the direct costs associated with generating leads and converting those leads into customers. In short, this is where the majority of your sales and marketing expenses will be tracked. While I understand that many online businesses see most of their expenses as being related to sales and marketing, not all of those expenses have a direct link. The word *direct* is key here. The majority of the expenses under the lead and conversion pillar will go up and down as revenue fluctuates. For an expense like advertising, the more money you spend on it, the more your revenue should go up too (assuming your ads are actually working well). For an expense like merchant fees, it will only increase if you make more sales (merchant accounts take a cut of every sale you make). With both of these examples, there is a direct link between the expense and the revenue increasing or decreasing together.

The Most Common Lead and Conversion Expenses

The most common expenses under this pillar are advertising, advertising managers, affiliate expenses, collections, marketing, merchant fees, and sales commissions. Let's explore each in a bit more detail.

Advertising

Any sort of ad buy is categorized under this expense pillar. For online businesses, social media advertising is by far the most popular. Other common advertising options for online businesses are podcasts, blogs, trade magazines, newspapers, and conferences.

Advertising Manager

Ad managers are one of the few contractors that we do not categorize under the labor pillar. That is because ad managers typically charge based on how much ad spend they are managing for your business. That means if your ads are doing well and you want to increase your ad spend, the cost of your ad manager will go up too. It is also helpful to categorize your ad manager expenses under the lead and conversion pillar so you can more easily see what you are spending on your ads and ad manager together.

Affiliate Expenses

If your business leverages affiliates to help you sell your offers, then all affiliate expenses would be categorized here. The more sales your affiliates make for your business, the higher your affiliate expenses will be because they typically take a percentage of each sale they make for your business.

Collections

Collections agencies help you collect payments from clients and customers who are past due on their payments. They typically take a cut of every dollar they recover for your business. That means the more money your collections agency collects for you, the higher your collections expense category will be.

Marketing

Any general marketing expenses would go under this category. While online businesses focus a lot of their resources on marketing, this category rarely lists many expenses. Common marketing expenses for online businesses are promotional materials (merch, business cards, printed marketing materials, and the like), networking events, and props for video production.

Merchant Fees

If your business utilizes a merchant provider like Stripe or PayPal, they will take a percentage of each sale you make as their fee for processing the payment. If your bookkeeper is properly reconciling your merchant accounts, then they should be tracking these fees on your profit and loss statement. If they are not tracking merchant fees, then it is a sign that they do not have much experience working with online businesses or that they are cutting corners to save time doing extra work.

Sales Commissions

Similar to ad managers, sales commissions are one of the few labor costs that do not go under the labor pillar. That is because most sales professionals take a cut of every sale they make (their percentage can vary depending on what they are selling), which means the more they sell, the more your sales commission expenses increase too.

One More Note About This Pillar

Much to the dismay of online business owners and their finance teams, most marketing tactics do not have a clear return on investment. Things like social media marketing, content marketing, and search engine optimization (SEO) are all super common marketing strategies but demand a long-term commitment of time and money before seeing a payoff. This usually means there is less of a direct connection between revenue increasing in conjunction with investments in these types of expenses (at least not to the same degree as ad managers and sales commissions). The other connection across these marketing strategies is that the expenses associated with them are almost always related to labor, be it contractors, agencies, or employees. This is why we recommend putting these types of expenses under the labor pillar instead of the lead and conversion pillar.

Lead and Conversion Pillar Metrics

Not every online business needs to invest heavily into their lead and conversion pillar to grow. So if you reviewed all of the expenses under this pillar, and the only one you can relate back to your own online business is merchant fees, then please know that is totally fine. For everyone else, it is crucial that you understand when you are investing too much money into lead and conversion expenses. Many of these expenses can be revenue drivers for your business, but if they are driving revenue at the expense of profitability, then it is important that you address this sooner than later.

Here are the ranges we like to see our clients stay within for the lead and conversion pillar.

Ideal Range

20% or less of total revenue

As this range suggests, I prefer online businesses to be spending 20% or less of their revenue on the lead and conversion pillar. Over the years, I have seen the other profit pillars become more expensive and more vital for the long-term success of an online business—most notably, the labor pillar. That means if your business is spending too much money on sales and marketing expenses, you will have a much tighter budget for team, offer delivery, and operations.

Sustainable Range

21-35% of total revenue

Some online businesses can operate with a small team and have little need for more sophisticated internal operations, especially if the offer is very easy to fulfill and the business operations are highly automated. When this is the case, I have seen online businesses spend upwards of 35% of their revenue on lead and conversion expenses and still maintain a 30% profit margin or better. Just know that this is less common than ever, but still doable for certain online businesses.

Unsustainable Range

35% or more of total revenue

Back in 2014 when I was first exposed to online businesses, it was more common to see businesses who were able to spend 40–50% of their revenue on lead and conversion expenses and still have a profit margin of 30% (to be fair, most were closer to 20%). This proved to be unsustainable though. These online businesses were spending so much on lead and conversion expenses that the owner did not have the budget needed to hire a team. When the stress and burnout of managing so much of the business on their own became too much, they either hired a team and prayed that they could drive enough revenue to pay for them (this never worked out) or they simply shut their businesses down. Both options sucked.

Lead & Conversion Pillar

The lead and conversion pillar consists of all the direct costs associated with generating leads and converting those leads into customers.

Advertising Ad Manager Affiliate Expenses Collections Marketing Merchant Fees Sales Commissions		**Ideal Range** 20% or less of total revenue
		Sustainable Range 21% to 35% of total revenue
		Unsustainable Range 35% or more of total revenue

Generating more leads and closing more customers is a desirable outcome, but as you can see from the metrics, there is a limit. The lead and conversion pillar will better help you discover where that limit is for your online business.

OFFER DELIVERY PILLAR

The offer delivery pillar consists of all the direct costs associated with delivering your offers to your customers and clients. Expenses that fall under this pillar will often have a direct connection to an increase or decrease in volume of your offer. That means if you sell more, you will also spend more money on the offer delivery pillar. The same would happen if the volume of your offer decreased. Your offer delivery pillar would decrease in cost as well. Online businesses that provide services, put on live events, or have a high touch component to their educational courses and programs will be more likely to have delivery expenses in their businesses.

The Most Common Offer Delivery Expenses

The most common expenses under the offer delivery pillar are: coaches / teachers / guest instructors, live event expenses, printing and fulfillment, and product development.

Coaches / Teachers / Guest Instructors

If you have an online education business and pay other coaches, teachers, or instructors to come into your program to support your customers, then those expenses would go under this expense category.

Live Event Expenses

If you sell tickets to live events that your business hosts, or you sell a digital product that includes access to a live event as part of the offer, then the expenses associated with your live events would go here. If you host free live events that are used to then upsell attendees to a paid offer, then you may want to consider tracking those live event expenses as a marketing expense under the lead and conversion pillar instead of under the offer delivery pillar.

Printing and Fulfillment

Some online businesses like to ship physical products to their clients and customers as part of their digital product or service. The expenses associated with shipping and fulfilling workbooks, books, journals, and welcome gifts can be categorized here.

Product Development

For online businesses that test their checkout processes by purchasing their own offers with a business credit card or debit card, those test transactions can be categorized here. Any other expenses related to developing a new offer and service can also be categorized here. If you are a content creator that makes money on YouTube and/or other similar social platforms, tracking video production costs under this category would work too.

One More Note About This Pillar

For agency owners and service providers, a case could be made for tracking the cost of the team members who serve your customers under the offer delivery pillar. After all, without these team members, you wouldn't be able to serve the customers. If these team members are contractors and not employees, then creating a custom category under the offer delivery pillar would be acceptable. If the team that serves your customers is made up of employees, then from a bookkeeping standpoint, it will be easier and cleaner to categorize them under the labor category. That said, I usually default to keeping these team expenses under the labor pillar in order to more easily assess your total team costs. Work with your bookkeeper to figure out what feels best for your business.

Offer Delivery Pillar Metrics

Similar to the lead and conversion pillar, not every online business will have offer delivery expenses. If you reviewed all of the expenses under this pillar, and you had little to no expenses to account for, please know this is not uncommon. Especially if what you sell is completely digital in nature. If offer delivery expenses are a big part of your business, then this pillar will be especially important to understand. Please keep in mind that the way you price and package your offer can have a profound effect on whether or not your business's growth will be stunted due to the offer delivery pillar.

Here are the ranges we like to see our clients stay within for the offer delivery pillar.

Ideal Range

10% or less of total revenue

The benefit of owning an online business is that the offer delivery process is so much easier than traditional businesses. Businesses selling physical products have to deal with manufacturing and logistics expenses, which, if not managed properly, can absolutely bring their business to its knees. That is why I like to see online businesses keep their offer delivery expenses to 10% or less.

Sustainable Range

11-20% of total revenue

For online businesses with higher touch components to their offer(s) that include individual or group support, seeing their offer delivery pillar get as high as 20% is not uncommon, especially if they have team members doing one-on-one work with their clients. That said, businesses like this tend to have lower marketing costs, which allows them to spend more on offer delivery expenses.

Unsustainable Range

21% or more of total revenue

The only times I have seen the offer delivery pillar get this high in an online business is if the owner went way over budget on their live event expenses or they created a lopsided revenue share program with their coaches / teachers / guest instructors. I am sure there are other examples of how an online business can see their offer delivery pillar surpass the 21% mark, but whatever the case, it is unlikely they will have a healthy profit margin after they account for their labor and operations pillar.

A Note for Service-Based Businesses

If you operate an online agency or service-based business and your team members who serve your clients are all contractors, then your offer delivery pillar could easily surpass 21%. If that is the case for your business, that is totally fine. You can get away with spending as much as 45% of your revenue on the team that services your clients and still be able to achieve a profit margin of 20% or better.

Remember that if the team members who work with your clients are a mix of employees and contractors, you will want to group all of your team under the labor expense pillar so you can more easily assess the state of your team costs.

I am personally a big fan of any online business that invests in delivering awesome results and experiences for their customers. It can be what separates a mediocre online business from an outstanding one. I can attest to this because Evolved Finance has put an intense focus around offer delivery. By monitoring your offer delivery pillar, you can make sure you are not overdelivering for your customers at the expense of your business's profitability.

Offer Delivery Pillar

The offer delivery pillar consists of all the direct costs associated with delivering your offer(s) to your clients and customers.

Coaches/Teachers/Guest Instructors

Live Event Expenses

Printing & Fulfillment

Product Development

Ideal Range
10% or less of total revenue

Sustainable Range
11% to 20% of total revenue

Unsustainable Range
21% or more of total revenue

LABOR PILLAR

The labor pillar includes the total cost of the contractors and/or employees that support your business. Unless you plan to be a freelancer/solopreneur for the rest of your career (which is totally fine if that is what you desire) and complete every project and task in your business, working with contractors and/or employees will be inevitable. No substantial business, online or otherwise, grows without the support of other people. The great thing about labor costs for online businesses is they do not always grow at the same rate as the business's revenue—at least not to the same extent as the lead and conversion and offer delivery pillars. Depending on the type of online business you have, labor expenses might be very easy to manage. It might also be the single most important expense you track and monitor in your online business for the sake of profitability due to the high cost of hiring a team.

The Most Common Labor Expenses

The most common expenses under this pillar are independent contractors, payroll, and team morale.

Independent Contractors

Aside from the few contractors that could potentially be categorized under one of the other pillars, the majority of the contractors you pay will likely end up under this category. I do not recommend lumping them all together in one category on your profit and loss statement, though. You can break down the contractors in your online business however you would like, but at Evolved Finance, we commonly use the following subcategories as a starting point:

- Assistants
- Copywriters
- Customer Service
- Design
- Operations Managers
- Photo/Video
- Podcast/Audio
- Project Managers
- Social Media Managers
- Tech / IT Support
- Web Development

Payroll

If you are utilizing a payroll provider to process payroll for yourself and/ or your team, then those transactions should be categorized here. It is important to know that your bookkeeper should be breaking out payroll taxes under the payroll category as well as the fees from your payroll provider. If they are not, then that might be a sign that they are inexperienced or cutting corners with their bookkeeping processes.

Below are the common subcategories we use under payroll for our clients at Evolved Finance.

- Employee Pay
- Employer Taxes
- Owner/Officer Pay
- Pay Period Fees

There are two things you may have noticed about these subcategories:

1. The owner's payroll is tracked separately from the rest of the employees' pay. The reason for this is to make it easy to monitor the owner's salary for accounting and financial analysis purposes.
2. There is only one main employee pay category to track the total amount of payroll going to employees. If you ever want more detail as to what each employee is being paid, you can run a payroll report from your payroll software to capture this information. I also recommend maintaining a spreadsheet with each employee's name, position, monthly pay, and yearly pay. Most bookkeepers would be able to help you with this process.

> *NOTE: For an online business operating outside of the United States, please know that payroll may need to be tracked differently on your profit and loss statement than what we suggest above.*

Team Morale

If your company purchases small gifts, hosts team retreats, or pays for any other team-building activities, these expenses can be categorized here.

One More Note About This Pillar

If you are wondering why I did not include your lawyer or accountant on the list of independent contractors, that is because these types of contractors go under the operations pillar as "legal and professional fees." This is customary for US-based businesses, but might not be necessary in other countries.

Labor Pillar Metrics

It can be tempting to want to spread your team costs across the other pillars based on the "departments" they work in. For instance, you may want to put all of the team members who work on marketing-related activities under the lead and conversion pillar. In all the years I have been looking at profit and loss statements, this has never been a helpful way to analyze an online business's financials. You can always break down your total labor expenses by function in a spreadsheet if the need arises. Otherwise, seeing your total labor costs as a percentage of your business's total income is the most useful and powerful way to gain quick insight into your team expenses. When a business owner can see that their team costs as a whole are too high, their instincts kick in and they can usually decipher why that is the case. There is no need to overcomplicate how you analyze your labor costs. Keep it simple!

Here are the ranges we like to see our clients stay within for the labor pillar.

Ideal Range

25% or less of total revenue

The most profitable non-service-based online businesses I have worked with are able to keep their labor costs under 25%. This does not mean they are underpaying or overworking their teams. It typically means one of two things: 1) that the business is in its early stages and the business owner is able to do a lot of the work in the business themselves or 2) the business owner has built great systems and processes that reduce the need for unnecessary team hires.

Sustainable Range

26-35% of total revenue

If your online business does not have to invest a lot of money into the other pillars, then spending more than 25% of your revenue on team costs can be completely sustainable. Many times, if an online business has labor costs in this sustainable range, 5–10% of the cost is the result of the owner's payroll salary (in the United States, this is part of a specific tax strategy), which means the cost of their team is not as high as it looks. Businesses with labor costs in this range might also be hiring in anticipation of their next phase of growth, investing in completing larger onetime projects (e.g., redesigning a website or building a new sales funnel), or trying to reduce the amount of time the owner is working in the business.

Unsustainable Range

36% or more of total revenue

When I see an online business with labor costs in this range, the most common reason is due to a slowdown in sales. The reasons for the dip in sales can vary greatly, but if that dip happens during a year during which there have been big investments in labor expenses for onetime projects or big hires were made in anticipation for revenue growth that never came, then the labor pillar can balloon pretty quickly. Whatever the case may be, any non-service-based online business that has labor costs creeping up toward 40% or more will likely struggle to keep profit margins anywhere near 30%.

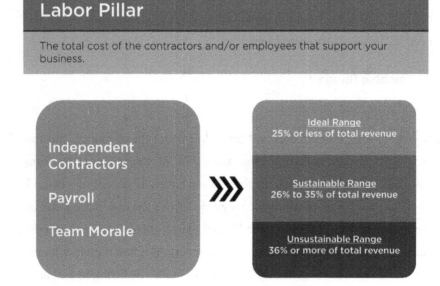

One thing I have always emphasized to our clients at Evolved Finance is that being hyperaware of your recurring monthly team expenses is more important than your onetime labor expenses. Obviously, expensive one-off labor projects can hurt your profit margin as much as any other expense, but they are rarely a sign of a bigger issue with the overarching business model. If an online business is regularly struggling with profitability due to the cost of their core team members, then that raises far more concerns around the financial model of the business.

A Labor Pillar Consideration for Service-Based Online Businesses

If you have a service-based online business, then the expectations for your labor expenses will look different. If you are still the main service provider to your clients, then your total labor costs should look pretty similar to the labor pillar metrics I just shared. If you have grown your business to the point that you now have team members providing the service to your clients instead of you, then your labor costs are going to look much higher. That is why in chapter seven I set the profit expectations for online service-based businesses at 20% or higher. The lower profit margin is due to the higher labor costs that are inherent in all service-based businesses.

If the total cost of the team providing the service to your clients and the team working behind the scenes of your business is less than 60%, then you should have a good chance of keeping your profit margin at 20% or higher. Just keep in mind that the closer your labor pillar is to 60%, the less money you will have to spend on other pillars while also maintaining a 20% profit margin.

OPERATIONS PILLAR

The operations pillar consists of all the smaller expenses in your online business that are not connected to any of the other three profit pillars. Some of the expenses under the operations pillar are business necessities and some of them are owner benefits and tax deductions. Rarely are any of the expenses in this pillar detrimental to the profitability of your business on their own, but when you add all of these expenses together, they can turn into a much larger piece of the pie.

The Most Common Operations Expenses

Please understand that the list of expense categories below is not comprehensive. Depending on the specific needs of your business, the accounting practices of the country you live in, and the preferences of your bookkeeper and accountant, there will be a wide variety of different types of expenses that can be tracked under the operations pillar. I tried to list the most common types of expense categories we use for our clients at Evolved Finance to give you and your bookkeeper a starting point.

The most common expenses under this pillar are automotive expenses, bank charges, charitable contributions, computer expenses, continuing education, insurance, legal and professional fees, meals, office expenses, travel, and more.

Automotive Expenses

Common expenses for this category are parking fees, gas for rental cars while traveling, and other auto-related business expenses. It is rare for online businesses to have many auto expenses, but if you believe your business model warrants writing off mileage expenses for your car or leasing a vehicle through your business entity, then confirm this with your accountant.

Bank Charges

This category is used to capture bank charges such as credit card and loan interest, annual fees for credit cards, wire fees, and overdraft fees.

Charitable Contributions

If you make charitable donations that are approved as tax deductions in your country, then those expenses would be categorized here. In the

United States, those organizations to which you donate typically need to have 501(c)(3) status to be deductible through your business.

Computer Expenses

This expense category can be used to capture hardware expenses (computers, phones, cameras, podcast gear, etc.), software subscriptions, and hosting/domain subscriptions. Make sure you talk with your accountant before making any large hardware purchases. If the item costs more than a certain amount, it might be considered an asset, which means your accountant will only be able to write off a portion of it for the current fiscal year. The threshold amount for hardware and equipment expenses can change from year to year depending on your country and any changes to tax laws, which is why I will emphasize again to check with your accountant if you have concerns.

Continuing Education

Any courses, coaching programs, consultants, conferences, or business book expenses would be categorized here.

Insurance

There are a variety of insurance products that can be purchased for business purposes. Common types are liability insurance, errors and omissions insurance, private practice insurance, key person insurance, and workers' compensation insurance. Any business insurance premiums should be categorized under this category.

Legal and Professional Fees

As I mentioned in the section about the labor pillar, legal and professional fees is one of the few categories under the operations pillar that includes contractor expenses (continuing education is the other one).

These contractors are most commonly going to be lawyers, accountants, and bookkeepers.

Meals

Purchasing meals while traveling for business is by far the most common type of meal expense for online businesses (assuming you are traveling overnight). It can also be appropriate to expense meals you have with clients, customers, and employees. For US businesses, know that you will not be able to write off the full amount of any meal. Please check with your accountant if you have any questions about your meal expenses.

Office Expenses

There are a variety of subcategories that we use for our clients under the office expense category. The most common ones are:

- Postage and shipping
- Rent (if you have an office space or are writing off a portion of the home you rent)
- Repairs and maintenance
- Small office furniture
- Supplies
- Utilities

Please note that if you work from a home office, you will want to get on the same page with your accountant about running your personal rent, personal utilities, and large office furniture expenses through your business.

Travel

If you travel for business, the expenses associated with your travel would be categorized here. At Evolved Finance, the subcategories we use most often are:

- Airfare
- Hotel
- Transportation

Other Common Operations Expense Categories

As I mentioned at the start of this section, your bookkeeper or accountant will likely use a variety of different operations expense categories. Just because they are not listed in greater detail in this book does not mean it is wrong to use them. Some of these expenses are very "accountant-y" in nature, so I do not want to spend time discussing them in greater detail. Just know that expense categories like the ones below are very common in the accounting world:

- Amortization
- Business taxes
- Dues and subscriptions
- Depreciation expenses
- Gifts given
- Licenses and permits

Operations Pillar Metrics

There is only one operations pillar expense that I regularly see online businesses spend enough money on that it negatively impacts their profitability, and that is continuing education. Otherwise, if the operations pillar is having a negative impact on profit, it is often the case that the business owner is spending a moderate amount of money across a number of operations expenses. The most common expenses are travel, legal fees, rent, software, and charitable contributions. It is rare that a single one of these expenses is the sole reason for an online business's profit struggles, but if more than one of these expenses gets out of hand at the same time, then it can definitely have an impact on profit margins. The good news is that even if your operations pillar is eating away at your profit margins, it is rarely because there are underlying issues with your business model. It just means you had some unexpectedly high onetime expenses (like a bill from your lawyer) or you are overindulging on owner benefits (such as incurring high travel costs from a nomadic lifestyle).

Here are the ranges we like to see our clients stay within for the operations pillar.

Ideal Range

15% or less of total revenue

Most of the online businesses I have monitored making over $500,000 per year sit in the 15% range for the operations pillar. The larger the business, the more likely they will keep the operations pillar somewhere around the 10–15% range. For businesses generating less than $500,000 per year in revenue, there is a higher chance that they surpass the 15% mark.

Sustainable Range

16-25% of total revenue

For online businesses making less than $500,000 per year, it is not uncommon to see their operations pillar over 15%. A large investment in continuing education, writing off a portion of their rent, or a heavy year of traveling can push them into this "sustainable range." The good news is that businesses of this size are not usually spending a ton of money in their other pillars yet, so they can afford for their operations pillar to be in the sustainable range.

Unsustainable Range

26% or more of total revenue

Like all the other pillars, a dip in revenue for the year can cause the operations pillar to go beyond 25%, even if the dollar amount spent in this pillar is not a lot of money. That said, smaller businesses can easily push into this range simply by investing in an expensive coaching program. I have also seen nomadic online business owners spend so much on travel that they sacrifice their business's profitability. Some of the more generous online business owners I have worked with have made conscious decisions to make large donations to charitable organizations, pushing their operations pillar to 25% and beyond. Examples like these are why financial turmoil in this pillar is usually temporary or easily fixable.

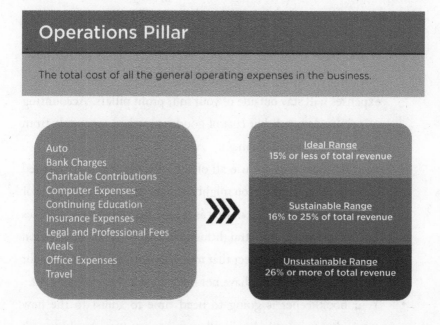

Understanding each of the four profit pillars and the metrics behind them will change the way you look at your business forever. Having a system for spotting and analyzing financial issues in your online business will significantly increase your chance of success as an online entrepreneur. But I want to go further than that. In the next chapter, I want to teach you how to think more strategically about your numbers, especially when your profitability metrics start to look concerning. If you can spot financial issues with your business as well as know how to pull the right levers to get your profitability on track, you will become the CEO you never even knew you had the potential to be.

TRANSITIONING TO THE PROFIT PILLARS SYSTEM

Here are a few more things to keep in mind as you work with your bookkeeper and/or accountant to transition to the Profit Pillars system.

- If you have true cost of goods expenses in your online business due to selling physical products, please know that those expenses will stay outside of your four profit pillars. Accounting principles demand that cost of goods is tracked separately from other expenses in a business.
- Your business will not use all of the subcategories I have listed for each pillar. In fact, you might not have any expenses in one or more of the profit pillars. That is totally fine. Online businesses can be so simple and straightforward that it is not uncommon for their finances to reflect that too. This is especially the case for smaller businesses that have not built up as many expenses yet.
- Your bookkeeper is going to need time to adjust to the new categories from this book. Plan to review your bookkeeper's

expense categorization more closely for the next few months to ensure the two of you are on the same page. If your bookkeeper is already not great about categorizing your expenses with your old profit and loss statement template, then they will need even more support from you during this transition.

- Unless your accountant deems that you have true cost of goods expenses in your online business, all of your business's expenses should be categorized under one of the main profit pillars. We have been using the four pillars with hundreds of clients at Evolved Finance and we've never run into an instance when a transaction could not be put in a subcategory under one of the four pillars.

- I want to reiterate that your online business might need to utilize expense categories under the four pillars that are not listed in this chapter. That is totally fine. As long as the categories fall under one of the pillars and make sense to you, your bookkeeper, and your accountant, then you are good to go. I do encourage you to use the categories I listed whenever possible, but just know that you do not need to rigidly abide to these expense category names if they do not make sense for your business.

- Your bookkeeper might not be thrilled that you want to change up the profit and loss structure because of the extra work it creates for them. Do not be surprised if they charge an extra fee for this work. It will be up to you to decide if you think that fee is reasonable or not. If your bookkeeper drags their feet on changing the profit and loss format or simply refuses to make any of the changes you request, then you might wish to interview for a new bookkeeper soon.

▪ **ACTION** ITEMS ▪

Now that we have covered all four of the profit pillars, what do you do with them?

The next step is to work with your bookkeeper to change the profit and loss template you are currently using to match what we have above. Your bookkeeper will need to do the following for this transition to work. If you are doing the bookkeeping for your business in a spreadsheet, then the steps are essentially the same.

1. **Add the four profit pillar names to your profit and loss statement as expenses.**

   It is as easy as it sounds. Your bookkeeper will log in to the bookkeeping software they are using to manage your books and add each of the four profit pillar names to the chart of accounts as expenses (among other things, the chart of accounts is where all the expense categories that your bookkeeper uses for your profit and loss statement live).

2. **Change and add expense names as needed.**

   Your bookkeeper is going to already have a long list of expense categories that they use for your profit and loss statement. After reading this chapter, you may realize that some of those categories do not make sense for your business anymore. You will want to review any of the categories currently being used for your profit and loss statement to see if you need to add new expense categories, delete old expense categories, or change the names of expense categories that are already being used. As part of this process, your bookkeeper will need to be prepared to recategorize expenses from earlier in the year into new categories. Most bookkeeping software makes it pretty easy to do this.

3. **Move all expense categories underneath the four profit pillars.**

   Each expense category that is being used for your profit and loss statement will need to be moved under one of the four profit pillar categories. That means all expenses on your profit and loss statement will now be subcategories under each of the four profit pillar expense categories.

4. **Audit your profit and loss statement.**

   Look over the details of your revised profit and loss statement with your bookkeeper to make sure that:

   - There are not any errant expenses floating outside of the four profit pillar expense categories.

   - Each expense category has the right expense transactions categorized inside of them.

5. **Generate your profit and loss statement with "% of income."**

   Now that the four expense pillars are integrated into your bookkeeping process, it will be important to generate your profit and loss statements so that there is a column that shows "% of income" for each expense. This is how you will be able to quickly and easily see how much of your business's revenue is going toward each pillar. Your bookkeeper should be able to run this type of financial report for you or show you how to do it yourself.

Once the transition is made, your bookkeeper should have an awesome profit and loss format to work from going forward. Over time, new expense categories might need to be added under the four pillars, but as long as you and your bookkeeper are working together to make sure transactions are going to the right places, you should have organized and easy-to-read profit and loss statements to look at each month.

If you are doing your own bookkeeping in a spreadsheet, move all of your expense categories under each of the four profit pillars, make sure those expense subcategories are named properly, and then audit your expense transaction categories to make sure the correct expense transactions are inside of them.

9

Using Your Profit Pillars to Fix Your Profitability

If you have been running your online business for a while now, you have probably discovered that a significant portion of your time is spent solving problems. This is an unavoidable part of entrepreneurship. If you are lucky enough to see your business grow and evolve, so will the types of problems you have to address and solve. This is why coaching and consulting for business owners is such a massive industry (I understand the irony of this statement as you read this book about solving a problem for your online business, but bear with me).

Entrepreneurs are regularly faced with problems in their businesses that they are not sure how to fix. From my experience, online business owners search for as much problem-solving support as any other type of small business. The numbers I have seen in my clients' businesses prove this. I have watched online entrepreneurs spend 15–20% of their revenue on coaching and courses, making continuing education their largest single expense category. That can look like a $200,000-a-year online business spending $30,000 on coaching and courses or an $850,000-a-year online business spending $130,000 on coaching and consultants. None of this is chump change.

If business problems were like a Lord of the Rings book, there would be one ring to rule them all: profitability. If you tell me about any single issue in your online business, I can show you how it ties back to your profitability. There are obviously an infinite number of issues that could arise in an online business. They can be as insignificant as a misspelled word on your website's home page or as significant as a 50% drop in revenue as compared to the previous year. What is important for you to understand as a business owner is how to prioritize which issues you address first based on how much impact they have on your profitability.

It should not be a surprise that looking at your numbers is the best way to get really good at solving problems in your business. This is why my business partner and I have spent so much less on coaches and consultants over the years as compared to our clients. Since I joined the business in 2014, we have only spent 1% of our revenue on coaches and consultants. The reason for this lies in our ability to use our financial data to both pinpoint issues in our business and give us clues on how to solve them.

In my experience, very few six- and seven-figure online business owners know how to pinpoint and define the issues in their business. The one thing they do know is if they have money in the business bank account or not. Unfortunately, this is not a sustainable way to run a business. This is where the four profit pillars can help. When used correctly, they can unveil the story behind your numbers, and understanding that story is one of the most powerful skills you can develop as a business owner.

During my time at adidas America, I worked closely with a number of really smart people in our finance department. Even though the department I worked in focused on product merchandizing, our team reported to a senior finance director. One of the most valuable pieces of advice he shared with me is the idea that there are stories behind all of the numbers in a business. If you look at a financial report and only see math, then you are missing half of the picture. The math is important, but the patterns and stories those numbers reveal are just as important. In a large corporation, it takes specialized financial expertise to know how to interpret those stories. For an online business, you only need your profit pillars to make sense of the numbers.

In the previous chapter, you were finally introduced to the four profit pillars. You not only learned which expenses make up each of the pillars, but you also learned what the preferred metrics are for each of the pillars. This knowledge is helpful for two reasons:

1. You now have a framework for organizing your profit and loss statement in a more meaningful way.
2. You now have the ability to identify precisely where issues lie in your profitability.

The ability to find issues in your online business is extremely valuable, but simply discovering an issue does not automatically fix it. For instance, if you know your labor profit pillar is way too high, but you do not know what to do about it, then you cannot expect to fix it. That is why my goal for this chapter is to share the most common reasons the expenses in each profit pillar can get too high. On top of that, I also want to review the most common ways you can boost profitability without cutting back on costs.

For many of you, this chapter will offer a solution to a profitability issue in your business that will be a perfect fit. It will be like I wrote that particular section of the book just for you. For others, it might not be as easy. While I wish this book could provide the exact solution every possible online business might need, that is just not a realistic expectation. That is why I encourage you to read this chapter in its entirety, even if you are reading about issues that are not relevant to your business. My hope is you will get a sense for the strategic thought process that goes into identifying and solving problems in your business through the use of the four profit pillars, and flex your own strategic business muscles to discover and solve any unique issues in your online business.

I am legitimately excited for what you are about to learn. Let's dive in!

WHEN REVENUE IS THE PROBLEM

The profit pillars framework revolves around managing the expenses in each of the four pillars so you can generate more profit. The thing is, sometimes your profit pillars are not the issue. Your revenue is. That is why before we jump into each of the pillars, I want to discuss revenue and sales.

If your profit is not where you want it to be, revenue might be the issue. Some signs of this might be:

- All four of your profit pillar metrics are in the unsustainable range but you do not see how you can cut back on any of your expenses (common for new or small online businesses).
- Your business was profitable in the past, but despite your expenses staying the same, profits have decreased.
- Your profit margin percentage looks great (30% or better), but the actual dollar amount of your profit is not enough to allow you to quit your full-time job or pay your personal bills.

If any of these scenarios strike a chord with you, then you probably need to focus on driving more sales.

There are thousands of books on sales and marketing, and while I am not a newbie when it comes to these topics, they are not my area of expertise. If you see me publish a book on sales and marketing in the future, then there might be a glitch in the matrix. That said, I have seen our clients at Evolved Finance learn a lot of hard lessons about generating revenue for their online businesses. Here are some of the most valuable ones I want to pass along to you in hopes that they give you some perspective on your revenue-generating activities.

No Launches or Promotions, No Revenue

Launches and promotions are the most profitable way to generate revenue that I have seen in the online space. If your business relies on launches or promotions to drive the majority of your revenue, then it would seem obvious that if you cut back on launching and promoting that your business will generate less revenue. For a lot of online business owners, however, the launch and promotional process can be so draining and tedious that they look for other ways to generate sales that are more automated or less labor intensive. While it is 100% possible to make sales in other ways, I have never seen an online business owner completely move away from live launches and promotions without taking a significant hit in sales. Instead of asking how you can launch or promote less, perhaps it would be more prudent to ask how you can make your launches less draining and stressful.

You Need to Increase Your Prices

There are times when I have seen an online business have plenty of paying customers and clients, but their revenue suffers because they are pricing their offer(s) too low. This is why pricing is absolutely critical to the success of your business model. If you are not charging enough money to match the value of your offer(s), then your profit pillar metrics will never look healthy no matter how much you cut back on your expenses. If you know your pricing strategy is hurting your top and bottom lines, then there are numerous books, coaches, and consultants that can offer advice and support.

Focus on Getting Good at Selling One Thing

When it comes to the quantity of offers you sell, less is more. I have seen many online entrepreneurs fall into the logic of "If I can make money selling one offer, I will make even more money selling secondary offers." This might be the case for your online business in the short term, but it can bite you in the butt for the long term. The more offers you have to sell, the more complex your online business becomes. The more complex your online business becomes, the more expensive it is to run your business. The more expensive it is to run your online business, the less profitable it will be.

When I see online businesses narrow down their offerings and really commit to getting good at selling one or two main offers, two positive things happen:

1. Their marketing messaging becomes more effective because they stay focused on learning how to sell their flagship offer(s) instead of confusing their audience by constantly trying to sell them new things.
2. Their business becomes more streamlined, focused, and profitable because they are not having to build systems and processes around all of the new offers they are trying to both create and sell every year.

Sometimes it makes total sense to create new offers or have to pivot away from old offers as your business grows and you and your team learn to better serve your customers, but if you are constantly making new offers instead of getting good at selling the one or two offers you have already had success with, you might be limiting the revenue potential of your online business.

Your Offer Might Not Be as Good as You Think It Is

Creating any sort of offer to sell online is not easy, but depending on the competition in your market, simply creating a "good enough" offer will only take you so far. Whether the offer you sell is good enough to get you to $50K a year or $200K a year, unless you are willing to take a hard look at how well your offer delivers on its promise to your customers/client/viewers, you will likely hit a peak only to watch your revenue eventually decline. Do not underestimate the importance of product development even after you have created the first iteration of your offer. Learning how to serve your customers/audience better is an ongoing process that never stops unless you allow it to.

Do Not Neglect Your Email List

One of the most foundational pieces of online marketing strategy is to build an email list. It does not matter if you are a musician, a freelancer, or a business coach. Your email list is one of the most valuable marketing assets inside of your business. Despite how ubiquitous this strategy may be, neglecting their email list is one big mistake I have seen some of our clients make over the years. This often happens because they get so focused on finding new leads or working on other areas of their business that they forget to cultivate a relationship with the leads that are already on their list. One of the best ways to drum up revenue for any online business is to reconnect with your email list and get your offer(s) in front of them again. Did somebody say "launch"?

If Life Happens, Reset Your Expectations

It is easy to forget that business owners are human beings who have lives outside of their businesses. Over the years, I have watched our clients become first-time parents, care for sick family members, deal with their own health issues (both mental and physical), go through break-ups and divorces, as well as experience a multitude of other personal challenges and milestones that might interfere in their abilities to run their businesses. In these instances, business owners cannot magically duplicate themselves so they can split time between their business and personal lives. There are times when your business comes second, which might mean your business generates less revenue. As long as your revenue expectations match the time and energy you have available to give to your business, then there is zero shame in taking space to deal with life as a human.

WHEN LEAD AND CONVERSION EXPENSES ARE THE PROBLEM

I want to start off by saying that not every online business needs to make big investments in their lead and conversion expenses in order to see their businesses grow. Content and social marketing are two of the most popular ways I have seen online businesses grow their audiences/ leads, and both strategies involve more labor expenses than lead and conversion expenses. Also, a lot of online businesses are able to close sales via a landing page or email sequence, so there is no need for a sales-person to close sales. Online service businesses usually get their sales from referrals and word of mouth, so their lead and conversion pillar can be especially nonexistent because there are no costs associated with that marketing strategy.

However, I have seen a number of online businesses invest heavily into lead and conversion expenses to grow their businesses over the years. They are typically trying to accomplish one or more of the following strategies:

1. Use paid advertising to drive leads to their cold traffic sales funnel.
2. Use retargeting ads during launches and promotional activities to increase sales conversion.
3. Use paid advertising for email list building so they can build a larger pool of leads to launch and promote their offers to.
4. Utilize commissioned salespeople to close their high-ticket offer(s) more effectively.
5. Leverage affiliate relationships to bring their offer(s) to new audiences.

The lead and conversion pillar can be a double-edged sword. Making investments in certain expenses under this pillar can lead to more sales and revenue growth, but they can demolish profitability along the way too. Remember when we talked about the two games you play as an entrepreneur in chapter three? Investing in this pillar with revenue growth as your only priority is a surefire way to lose at playing Game #2 (managing your cash flow).

If the metrics behind your lead and conversion profit pillar are not where you would like them to be, here are some things to consider.

You Are Not Tracking Your Advertising Metrics Properly

When the advertising expense category starts to balloon in an online business, the first thing I ask the owner is how they are tracking their advertising metrics. If they are only tracking the metrics around their ads and not the metrics for the entirety of their sales funnel, they are likely throwing money away. Is it important to know what your cost per click is? Of course. But you should also be tracking the metrics for all of the conversion events from the moment someone clicks your ad all the way through your sales funnel to the purchase of your offer. An experienced ad manager or ad agency will do this by default, but if you are working with a less experienced ad manager or you are trying to run ads yourself, you might be missing key insights to help you fix the parts of your sales funnel that are not converting.

You Are Trying to Send Paid Traffic to a Mediocre Sales Funnel

Over the years, we have had a number of clients who looked to paid advertising to speed up their revenue growth. There is nothing wrong with wanting to do this, but many of these business owners were not that great at selling their offer to a warm audience yet. Their conversion numbers were okay, but it was obvious that they had not yet perfected their sales and marketing processes. When they started investing in cold traffic advertising, their conversion rates got even worse (which is often the case with cold traffic), yet they spent thousands of dollars a month hoping things would change. If selling your offer to your warm audience still feels like pulling teeth, then you may want to consider pausing your ad spend until you improve the conversion rate of your warm traffic first.

Your Advertising Manager Is Taking Too Big of a Cut

Many ad managers price their services by charging a flat monthly fee plus a percentage of the total ad spend they manage. Depending on the manager (or agency), that percentage can range anywhere from 10–20%. This can have a massive impact on the total cost of your ad management, especially as your ad spend increases. If your ad manager is not able to provide a return on investment from your ad spend that covers their costs as well, then it is time to either renegotiate their rate or look for a new ad manager.

Your Affiliate Partners Are Taking Too Large of a Cut

Affiliate marketing is when you partner with another business to promote and sell your offer to their audience. In return, you give your affiliate partner a percentage of each sale they help you make. Some of the biggest names in the online business space grew their revenue and their audiences through affiliate marketing. It is a relatively risk-free way to make sales (far less risky than advertising), but depending on the affiliate agreement you have with your partners, it can do big damage to your profitability. For many years, the standard affiliate agreement has been to give your affiliate partners 50% of each sale you make to their audience. This has never felt fair to me. If you are the one paying for the merchant fees, customer service, promotional materials, and offer delivery expenses, your own cut should not be the same as your affiliate partner's cut. If a 50-50 affiliate agreement is having a negative impact on your profitability, you may want to consider offering a 20–40% commission instead.

Your Sales Team Is Taking Too Large of a Cut

Let me start off by saying that giving sales professionals a percentage of every sale they make (also known as a sales commission) is common for many different industries outside of the online business space. The commission structure you agree to with your internal or external sales team can have a massive impact on the profitability of your business. If you are giving away too big of a cut, you will always struggle with profitability no matter how many sales they close for your business. There are a few things you need to consider if your sales commissions are eating up too much of your cash.

- If you want to keep a commission structure in place for your sales team, you might need to renegotiate the commission structure to a lower percentage of each sale. This is not an easy conversation to have, but a necessary one if your commission percentage is more generous than your business can afford it to be.

- Instead of a commission structure, you can offer a base salary with performance bonuses for hitting certain sales milestones. This allows your sales team to have more secure incomes while still being incentivized to go out and hit their milestones. This type of compensation structure only works if the salesperson/people are not part of a sales agency, as agencies need a commission structure for their business models to work.

- I have seen a number of salespeople who demand they are paid full sales commissions even if your customer requests a refund or defaults on their payment plan. Aside from being unfair, this sort of agreement with your sales team can make your sales commissions far more expensive. If you have an agreement like this in place with your sales team, you may want to consider renegotiating this part of the contract.

- Businesses that need salespeople to sell their products or services have to price their products so they can afford to not just pay for their sales team's commissions, but to also cover the other expenses of running the business. If your commissions are hurting your profitability, the commission structure might actually be fine, but the pricing of your offer is the issue.

WHEN OFFER DELIVERY EXPENSES ARE THE PROBLEM

When I joined Evolved Finance back in 2014, the Profit Pillars system was just a twinkle in my eye. If current-day Parker could go back in time and show the 2014 Parker the profit pillars, he would likely be most confused by the offer delivery pillar. The reason being that the majority of our clients in 2014 did not have any direct costs associated with delivering their offers. They either sold stand-alone courses with no live support, offered one-on-one coaching or consulting services, or they received sponsorship and royalty income.

As the online business landscape has evolved and become more competitive, I have seen an increased number of our clients with online education and coaching businesses invest more of their revenue into the offer delivery pillar. In order to stand out and really deliver results for their customers and clients in a more competitive landscape, they have had to put more resources into their customer experience. That has typically come in the form of investing money into the people who coach and teach their students (coaches / teachers / guest instructors) as well as investing in live events.

I have seen more and more businesses struggle to manage the expenses in this pillar in recent years. It can be tricky to solve issues with the expenses in this pillar because they are closely tied to how your offers are structured,

which means you have to more deeply examine if the way you are supporting and serving your customers is sustainable. Whatever the case may be
for your business, the suggestion below should get you on the right track.

Your "Price-to-Support Ratio" Is Not Sustainable

For online businesses with education-based offers, it is very common to
offer some form of live educational support for the customers who have
access to your course, coaching program, or membership site. That live
support might come from coaches, teachers, or instructors who work
for your company as contractors. If the cost of these team members is
starting to have an impact on your profitability, then the price you are
charging for your offer versus the level of support your customers are
receiving might be out of whack. In simpler terms, it means you are
including too much high-touch support in your offers relative to the
price you are charging.

There are two ways you can fix this issue.

- **Increase the price of your offer(s) to better reflect the level of
  support your students receive.** This is usually an appropriate
  course of action if you know what you teach or coach demands
  a lot of accountability and hand-holding for your customers,
  which warrants keeping or increasing the amount of live support included in your offer(s).
- **Reduce the amount of support your students receive to better
  reflect the price of your offer(s).** This is usually an appropriate
  course of action if you know your customers can get results from
  your offer without the need for so many high-touch components. This might mean reducing the amount of live support
  that is included in your offer(s).

A Revenue- or Profit-Sharing Agreement Is Eroding Your Profits

For most online education businesses, the owner is almost always the talking head for any of the educational materials they sell. Over the years, though, I have seen more online educators hire outside subject matter experts to create educational materials like courses and e-books that the business then promotes and sells. While I have no issue with this type of product development arrangement, the compensation for the outside expert often comes in the form of some sort of revenue- or profit-sharing agreement. This means the outside expert receives a portion of each and every sale, even though they are doing nothing to promote or market the offer themselves. These types of agreements almost always disproportionately benefit the outside expert, as they are only making onetime efforts to create the educational material being sold, while the business owner has the ongoing responsibility of promoting and selling the offer while also taking on all of the expenses of running the business. If your offer delivery pillar metrics are looking unhealthy due to an agreement like this, you may need to renegotiate your revenue- or profit-sharing agreements.

You Are Not Turning a Profit on Your Live Events

When you run an online business, live events can be an awesome opportunity to cultivate a deeper connection with your customers, clients, and followers whom you have only interacted with in an online environment. Unfortunately, the expenses associated with putting on live events can quickly erode your margins if you do not manage them closely. The key to making your live events a success is to plan ahead and set a budget for how much the event will cost. Once you feel confident about what the event will cost you, you can then calculate how many tickets you need to sell in order to turn a profit on the event. If you are hoping to break even on the ticket sales but make your profit through upselling attendees into one of your other offers, then how many sales do you need to close to make the live event worth the time and effort? This entire process can be very risky since you typically have to front the cost of the event before you start selling tickets, so planning ahead and creating a strict budget is one of the best ways to reduce that risk.

WHEN LABOR EXPENSES ARE THE PROBLEM

Managing the cost of a team of contractors and/or employees is one of the most difficult financial tasks an online business owner can face. By not investing in your team, you are essentially saying you do not want your business to grow. By overinvesting in your team, you can cause massive profitability issues that can be difficult to fix. Neither of these extremes is desirable, but finding the middle ground takes intention and strategy.

The main reason managing team costs can be so tricky is because there is no set template or road map that every online business can simply copy and paste. The hires you make for your business will be dependent on the business skills you lack, the type of business model you are running, and your operational priorities. For instance, a content creator's first hire might be a video editor whereas a course creator might need their first hire to be a virtual assistant. These might seem like obvious examples, but I have seen numerous online businesses lose operational focus and end up with a large team of contractors and employees where much of the work they are doing is not business critical.

If your labor pillar is the main reason you are not hitting your profitability goals, then here are some of the most common reasons I have seen for labor expenses getting too high.

You Planned for Growth That Never Happened

Very few online entrepreneurs would start their businesses if they did not think the business was going to grow. While some are more aggressive with their growth estimates than others, every online business owner should have a plan for how they are going to acquire new customers. Where I have seen business owners make mistakes is bringing on a bunch of new contractors and/or employees before the business can afford it, with the expectation that their revenue will catch up with their labor costs down the road. If that growth does not come, or at least come fast enough, profit suffers as they try to pay for a team they cannot afford. This becomes more devastating when the business owner is in denial about their revenue and goes into debt in order to keep their team intact. If you hired too quickly or too soon in your own business, it is better to accept this reality and take action to lower your labor expenses before you deplete your savings or take on debt.

You Are Not Willing or Able to Do More of the Work Yourself

While it might sound "judge-y" to imply that you are not willing to work more in your business, the truth is that life circumstances might not allow you to work as much as you would like. Health issues, mental burnout, family emergencies, or big life changes might leave you leaning on your team to pick up some of your slack. There is zero shame in needing the support of your team, but you do need to accept that your business will likely be less profitable as you lean on them to manage more of your responsibilities. The math is pretty simple here. The more a business owner works in their business, the less they have to pay other team members to do their work for them. The less a business owner works in their business, the more they have to pay their team to take on the owner's responsibilities. Obviously, many business owners hope to grow their companies to the point that they can truly afford a team of employees and contractors who can manage the daily needs of the business without going into financial ruin, but if life circumstances force you to do this before the business is financially ready, you will likely have to accept a much smaller profit margin as you pay your team to run your business.

You Are Working with Too Many Contractors and Agencies

Online businesses can get away with hiring contractors and agencies more than any other type of business. Depending on the type of online business you own and the amount of revenue it generates, it might be totally acceptable to work primarily with contractors. However, if your labor expenses are getting unruly, and you do not have any employees on your team, you might be paying the price of only working with contractors and agencies. It is important to remember that these are fellow business owners you are working with, which means they need to charge an hourly rate or a monthly retainer that allows them to turn a profit. This might be a fine arrangement to have with your accountant, lawyer, bookkeeper, or project-based contractor. However, it is only a matter of time before it is no longer a financially viable arrangement for the team members that manage the daily operations of your business. If your labor expenses are too high, and your team is primarily made up of contractors and agencies, it might be time to replace some of those team members with full-time or part-time employees.

You Brought on Higher-Level Team Members Than You Actually Needed

A big hiring mistake I have seen many online businesses make is hiring people into their businesses at too high of a level. Oftentimes, the business owner is feeling overwhelmed and unorganized, so they want to hire magical unicorns to clean up their messes and make sense of their chaos. One out of ten times they find that person and everything works out perfectly. Nine out of ten times, the owner ends up with high-paid employees that the business cannot afford. If your labor expenses are high, but your team is small, there is a chance that you are paying team members too much money for the level of work they are doing in your business. If you need high-level, critical-thinking team members to manage a business making less than a million dollars a year in revenue, you might need to work on streamlining your systems and operations instead of hiring expensive employees to deal with an unnecessarily complex business.

You Are Trying to Work on Too Many Projects at Once

Running a business is all about effectively managing two resources: time and money. As your business grows, you will get busier and have less time to work on all the things in the business that need attention. You will likely have more money, so you will use the money to hire other people who can spend their time on addressing the various needs of the business. The more things you are trying to do in your business at once, the more money or the more time you will need to accomplish them. While this might seem rather straightforward, I have seen many online business owners fail at managing these two resources. One of the most common reasons for this is they are trying to do too much in the business at once. They are selling too many offers, working on too many projects, and trying to make too many improvements all at the same time. This all adds up to a business with unsustainable team expenses. If your labor expenses have gotten too high and you also have a long list of different employees and contractors working in your business, you are likely stretching your resources too thin. If you are willing to get your team and business more focused, you might find that your revenue will grow faster while your expenses stay lower. That is a great recipe for profit. Use your resources wisely and focus on the aspects of your business that matter most. If you do not know what those things are, make it a priority to figure it out.

Your Owner's Salary Is Inflating Your Labor Expenses

For many of the online businesses we work with, the owner is paid as an employee of the business. That means a payroll service takes money out of the business checking account, processes all of the necessary taxes, and then deposits the net amount in the owner's personal checking account. There are a number of reasons you would want to go through this effort, but for the sake of the labor pillar, it is important to understand that your owner's salary will inflate your labor expenses. Depending on the size of your salary, it could inflate it by a nominal amount or by a significant amount. If your labor pillar looks high because of your owner's salary, and it does not make sense to lower your monthly salary, then you might need to just accept your labor metric pillar will look too high. You can always subtract your salary from your labor pillar if you want to get a more realistic idea of your team costs. For instance, if your labor pillar is at 40%, but your salary makes up 15% of it, then your actual team costs are only 25% of your business's revenue (40 - 15 = 25).

WHEN OPERATIONS EXPENSES
ARE THE PROBLEM

As I have mentioned before, the operations pillar is rarely a major concern for me when I analyze an online business. Aside from a handful of categories like computer expenses, legal and professional fees, and office expenses, most operating expenses are not integral to the daily functioning of your business. At least not to the same extent that the expenses in the other three profit pillars are. All of that to say, the expenses under the operations pillar can still have a negative impact on your profitability, but the solutions to fixing the expenses under this pillar are typically more straightforward. That can sometimes mean cutting back on spending for some of these expense categories, but it can also mean accepting that you are okay with some of these expenses being high due to your life circumstances or your personal values. This will make more sense as you read through some of the examples below.

You Are Paying a Lot of Interest on Business Loans and Credit Cards

I am a huge believer that online businesses should avoid taking out business loans or using credit cards to pay for things the business cannot afford. That said, I have known enough online business owners who have used debt to get through hard times to understand that desperate times call for desperate measures. If the interest on your debt is eating up a sizable chunk of your revenue each month, there are a few things to consider.

- Tighten up your personal budget. The more money you can leave in the business to pay down its debts, the faster you can dig yourself out of your hole.
- Pay off high-interest debt first. Credit cards tend to have the highest rates, but there are a number of predatory lenders who will give out loans to small business owners with shockingly high interest rates.
- If you have credit cards you can afford to pay off right now, you can choose to tackle those first, even if you have credit cards with higher interest rates.
- Do not neglect saving for taxes as you pay down your debt. Governments tend to be less forgiving about not paying taxes than your creditors are about collecting debt.

Debt sucks, but you can get through it. I have seen many online business owners dig their way out of debt and run very profitable businesses. If they can do it, so can you.

Charity Is Important to You

The charity expense category is one that represents your personal values. I have seen a number of online business owners be extraordinarily generous with their charitable donations. They consciously make the decision to reduce their profit in order to give money to organizations they believe are making a positive impact on the world. If you are one of these people, I salute you. I still want to offer a couple nuggets of wisdom though.

- Make sure your charitable contributions are actually tax deductible. In the United States, a charity has to be designated as a 501(c)(3) for your donations to be tax deductible. If you have a business outside of the United States, please talk to your accountant about how charitable contributions work in your country.

- What do flight attendants always tell the passengers on a plane during their safety briefings? Put on your own oxygen mask before helping someone else to put on theirs. The idea being that if you pass out from a lack of oxygen, you will not be able to help the people around you who might need your help to put on their masks too. This same concept applies to your business. If you are giving too much of your profit to charity now, you may actually be stunting the growth of your business in the future. A financially stable business can donate a lot of money over time. A financially stunted business may only be able to donate for a short period of time and then never be able to do it again.

You Are Not Willing or Able to Do More of the Work Yourself

At Evolved Finance, we work with a lot of coaches and online educators. These types of business owners love to invest in coaching and education for themselves too. I have seen a number of their investments in continuing education provide massive returns. The return does not always happen right away, but the right course or coaching program can truly make a difference in their business if the owner invests in education they actually need and puts in the work to execute on what they have learned.

On the flip side, I have seen our clients collectively spend millions of dollars on courses, conferences, coaching, masterminds, and memberships that made little impact on their businesses. There are three reasons this happens so often.

The biggest reason is time. Most business owners are busy, so when they invest in continuing education, especially in multiple programs at once, they quickly realize that they do not have the time to execute on what they have learned. This is essentially lighting money on fire.

I have also seen online business owners use courses and coaching to distract themselves from taking meaningful action in their businesses. Talking about their business or learning new strategies feels more comfortable to them than doing the work to actually show up in their business in the way the business needs them to in that moment.

Lastly, I have seen online business owners invest in continuing education when they should actually be using their money to hire contractors or employees to help them get more done within their businesses. They are so used to looking to coaches and experts to solve problems in their businesses that they forget hiring actual team members can often be a better solution to their issues.

You Are Dealing with Legal Troubles or Tax Problems

The legal and professional fee expense category is usually fairly predictable each year. However, there might be a year when your business needs some unexpected legal support from a business attorney or your accountant has to clean up some tax issues. While it is not fun to see these types of expenses reduce your profit, there typically is not much you can do to lower these costs when they happen. If these types of expenses are hurting your bottom line, you can at least find solace in the fact that they are onetime expenses that will eventually have an end.

You Are Traveling a Lot

One of the many great benefits to running an online business is you can work from anywhere. We have seen our clients at Evolved Finance work from different locations all across the world. While this level of freedom and flexibility is pretty awesome, it also costs money. I have seen a number of business owners spend enough on travel in their businesses that it has a significant impact on the business's profit. Luckily, there is an easy fix: travel less. That said, if being a nomadic entrepreneur is important to you, and you understand that you are spending money that the business could be reinvesting in many other ways (including your personal finances), then by all means, enjoy your travel without guilt.

You Spend a Lot of Money on Your Rent

One of the benefits of renting your home as a business owner is you get to write off a portion of your rent as a business expense. While this is a cool benefit of entrepreneurship, this is a good example of how personal financial decisions can have an impact on your business. For instance, we have had clients at Evolved Finance who sign leases for apartments in places like New York City and Los Angeles that were so high, the portion of their rent that they were running through their businesses was enough to put significant financial strain on their cash flow.

If you have a dedicated office space outside of your home that you pay rent on, that is a bit of a different story. It is not uncommon for online service providers and content creators to have office/studio spaces outside of their homes. If you have a business like this, and your rent is pushing your operations costs to unhealthy levels, you may want to consider finding a more affordable space, dropping your lease and moving to a fully virtual business model, or simply driving more revenue to better justify the cost of your space.

▪ ACTION ITEMS ▪

I want to acknowledge that this chapter might be asking you to make some really difficult choices in your business. While the concepts discussed in this chapter are not particularly difficult to understand, the realities of what you discover from putting this chapter into action might push you as a leader and business owner to act in ways that are new and uncomfortable. For instance, you might need to come to terms with financial decisions you can now see are unsustainable and holding back your business from thriving. It might mean having a difficult employment conversation with a team member that you truly care about as a person. It might even mean drastically changing the direction of your business after years of operating in a way that was comfortable to you and your team. Business ownership is hard, but I have seen so many entrepreneurs make really difficult decisions and ultimately have healthier businesses for it. I know you can too.

If you are analyzing your business through the lens of the four profit pillars for the first time, then congratulations! You are reaping the rewards of this book! If you have followed along with the action items from chapter eight, you should be receiving financial reports from your bookkeeper each month that allow you to see the metrics behind your four profit pillars. The goal now is to make reviewing and analyzing your numbers a monthly habit.

Here are some steps to help you along the way:

- **Make sure you and your bookkeeper agree about receiving your financial reports the same day each month.** If you are not getting these reports regularly, then you are missing out on opportunities to obtain financial feedback that will allow you to take swift action to resolve financial issues.

- **Carve out time on your calendar to review your financial reports and analyze your four profit pillars.** This should be a recurring meeting. Treat it like church.

- **For more accountability, invite other people to look at your reports with you.** If you need to pay your bookkeeper to review your financial reports with you in the beginning, then that is money well spent. If you need one of your team members to review the numbers with you, then invite them to your monthly recurring meeting as well. Looking at your reports with others can make the process a lot less intimidating and create accountability for not skipping out on looking at your numbers.

- **If your profitability is not where you want it to be, your first priority should be to assess which profit pillar(s) are the biggest culprits.** If you have multiple pillars causing profitability issues, address the pillar with the highest expenses first. Just keep in mind that you might not be able to cut many expenses and may need to focus on driving more sales instead.

- **Once you know which profit pillar(s) are the biggest issue in your business, dive deeper into the individual expense categories that are costing the business the most money.** Your bookkeeper can easily pull reports that will show you all of the individual transactions that make up any expense category on your profit and loss statement. You can also ask if your bookkeeper will teach you how to go into your bookkeeping software and find the data you need yourself.

- **Trust your instincts.** Once you have found the specific expense categories that are causing the profitability issues in your online business, it is time to start problem-solving. You can always reference this chapter to see if there are some ideas here for how to fix your specific profitability issues. Otherwise, you might need to brainstorm some potential solutions on your own or with your team. You might be surprised by the solutions you can come up with within your own company. If you are really stuck, though, hiring a coach or consultant is always an option as well.

10

How to Pay Yourself Without Breaking Your Business

One of the most appealing aspects of being an online business owner is the higher income ceiling that comes from entrepreneurship. Whatever career you had in the past, your online business very likely has the potential to make you more money than your old career ever could. Hell, you might already be making more money from your online business than you were in your previous job. Most of our clients at Evolved Finance are in this exact situation. What I find odd is how few online entrepreneurs want to admit that making money is a driving motivator for them. What they will say out loud is that their business has given them more freedom, flexibility, autonomy, the opportunity to pursue their passion, and the ability to make an impact. These are all awesome motivators and benefits of business ownership, but they are only possible if you are getting paid enough to pay your bills. Talk to any struggling entrepreneur and you will see how little they mention freedom or impact when they are barely scraping by.

So can we agree that paying yourself is an important part of being an online business owner? If you are underpaid or not being paid at all, your online business will not survive. Paying yourself should be a priority. After all, you are not running a charity; you are building an online business that can turn a profit and afford you whatever lifestyle feels right for you.

Before we move on, please do not confuse my desire for you to build a healthy income from your online business as me asking you to be greedy or selfish. I have seen many online business owners build real wealth for themselves while also paying their teams competitive salaries and delivering amazing results for their customers. Your wealth-building process does not have to include taking advantage of others. If you do it right, the growth of your business should mean more money for you, more money for your team, and more customers who are benefiting from your offers.

It is safe to say that if you have made it this far in the book, you are taking the financial side of your business seriously (or you are at least working toward doing so). You want an online business that can turn a profit and support your lifestyle. The profit pillars you have learned about in the previous chapters are there to help you make this a reality. As we have discussed already, the more profitable your online business, the more opportunity you will have to pay yourself a salary that is beyond anything you would have made in your past career.

Seems easy enough, right? The more profit in your business, the more you can pay yourself as the owner. Here is where things can get tricky. Unless you have a business with very consistent recurring revenue, you likely see your revenue fluctuate from month to month. If your revenue fluctuates, then chances are your profits fluctuate too. While this is a completely natural part of running an online business, it does make paying yourself a consistent salary more difficult if your profit looks wildly different from month to month.

The trap here is that when you have a month of low profits, you will pay yourself very little or nothing at all. When you have a high profit month, you cut yourself a big old check to make up for the months where you made jack-crap. There are some major issues with falling into this pattern.

- It becomes difficult to manage your personal finances when you are not sure how much money you are going to make each month.
- It becomes too easy to pull all of the profit out of your business to pay yourself each month and have no money left over to invest back into the business.
- During the months when you do not pay yourself enough, you put yourself in a scarcity mindset that is not conducive to long-term strategic thinking.

Fortunately, this is a trap you can 100% pull yourself out from. If your online business is generating enough profit to pay yourself a full-time income, then I can show you how to pay yourself a consistent salary each month while also making your cash flow much easier to manage. The benefits are massive.

- You can create a monthly salary for yourself that you can rely on and plan your personal budget around.
- You will have a financial runway in your business that will allow you to pivot and problem-solve when your business is under financial stress.
- You will have cash available to make big investments in your business without having to max out credit cards or take on loans.
- Your ability to make calm and rational long-term strategic decisions for your business will increase as you no longer operate from a place of scarcity and desperation.

Are you sold yet? Great! Let's dive in!

......

When it comes to paying yourself as a business owner, it might seem like your only goal is to pay yourself a consistent salary. This is indeed a great goal to have, but you also do not want your salary to be financially debilitating to your business. If you are always taking the majority of your profit and transferring it to yourself as part of your compensation, your business will never have the extra cash it needs to deal with unplanned expenses, navigate sudden dips in revenue, or jump on opportunities to invest back into your business to help it grow. In simpler terms, you need a consistent salary as well as a savings cushion in your business.

Here is how you accomplish this balance:

1. Decide on a consistent monthly salary.
2. Build up a business savings cushion.
3. Take bonuses when your business is sitting on more cash than it needs.
4. Increase your salary over time as your business is able to sustain new levels of profit.

You don't think I would just give you four steps and not explain any of them, right? Of course not! Let's dive deeper into how you can put these four steps into action.

HOW MUCH SHOULD YOUR MONTHLY SALARY BE?

There are two things you need to figure out in order to land on a consistent monthly salary for yourself.

- How much money can your business afford to pay you?
- How much money do you need personally to live?

To figure out how much your online business can pay you each month, I recommend calculating the average profit your business has generated over the last six months. This makes it easier to see how much your business can afford to pay you even if your profit fluctuates drastically throughout the year. Here is how you do this.

1. Add up the total amount of profit your business has generated over the past six months.
2. Divide your six-month profit total by six. You now have your average monthly profit!

Here is an example.

Let's say over the course of the last six months, my online business has generated $57,341 in total profit. To find the monthly average of this number, I divide it by six. This gives me a monthly average profit of $9,557.

Once you know what your average monthly profit is, you can then decide how much of that profit should be going to you as the business owner. Please note that if you are not paying yourself through payroll as the business owner, then your compensation will come entirely from your profit. If your business is paying you through payroll each month, though, then part of your monthly compensation will already be accounted for as an expense under the labor profit pillar, so your monthly salary will be a combination of what you take through payroll as well as what you take from your profits.

Now that you have calculated your average monthly profit, you will need to know if that monthly profit will be enough to pay you a salary that will support your lifestyle. This is where a personal budget becomes invaluable. If you skipped chapter four, I would recommend you go back and read it. I lay out an entire game plan for building a budget for your personal finances.

Once you have your personal budget worked out, you can then see if your business has the ability to support your personal financial needs. For instance, if your business is averaging $12,000 per month in profit, but you only need $6,000 to cover your personal bills, then your monthly salary would be easily supported by the business. If your business was only generating $5,000 per month in profit, but you still needed $6,000 per month to pay your bills, then you will need more income, be it from your business or from a side job, to make sure you can cover your business's tax bill as well as your monthly personal financial responsibilities.

Speaking of taxes, in most countries, your business will be taxed based on its profit. That means if you are averaging $10,000 per month in profit, anywhere from 20–50% will need to be saved for taxes. Your exact percentage will depend on a number of factors (federal tax brackets, state/provincial tax brackets, spouse's income, etc.), so talk with your accountant to figure out how much of your profit you personally need to save for taxes. I cannot emphasize the importance of this step enough. If your business is making enough to pay you what you need for your personal finances, but not enough to also pay your tax bill, then your business cannot actually afford to pay you your salary. Talk to your accountant!

Once you have your monthly salary locked in, the goal is that you do not pay yourself more than that salary if you have a really good month. Any extra profit will stay in the business until you build up a savings cushion. This cushion will be extremely important for stabilizing your cash flow and ensuring you can take your monthly salary even in the months when your profit is below your six-month average.

If you are barely making enough profit to pay your taxes and cover your owner's salary, then you need to understand that your business's savings cushion will stagnate unless you generate more profit. To fix this, you will have to do one or more of the following:

- Cut expenses in your business to boost your profits.
- Decrease your personal expenses so you can live on a smaller salary.
- Learn how to generate more revenue without your expenses increasing drastically so your profit can grow beyond just covering your salary. (This is the solution most entrepreneurs prefer. Go figure.)

Once you have your salary figured out, your next job is to set your business's savings goal.

HOW MUCH MONEY SHOULD YOU SAVE IN YOUR ONLINE BUSINESS?

When working with our clients at Evolved Finance, we recommend they save at least three months of expenses inside their businesses. To calculate this number for your business, do the following:

1. Add up the total amount of your business's expenses over the past six months. Yes, this will include the expenses under all four profit pillars.
2. Take the total of your expenses from the last six months and divide that number by six. This number is the average of your monthly expenses.
3. Now that you have your average monthly expenses for the past six months, multiply this number by three to calculate your three-month savings cushion.

Here is an example.

Let's say over the course of the last six months, my online business has spent $75,000 on all of my business expenses. To find the average of this number, I divide it by six. This gives me a monthly average of $12,500 in business expenses. In order to calculate the three-month savings cushion for my online business, I would multiply the $12,500 by three. This would give me a savings goal of $37,500.

Obviously, you can save more than three months of expenses if you would like, but I have found three months to be a nice happy medium for the majority of online businesses. It is enough of a runway that it gives most businesses enough time to address any issues that might cause profits to dip, but it is not such a long period of time that the business owner feels like they are holding on to an unnecessarily large amount of cash. All of that said, if you plan to make a larger onetime investment in your business, or you anticipate that your monthly expenses will be increasing significantly in the near future, then you may want to save more than just the three months of expenses.

It is important to keep in mind that your three-month savings cushion will be a moving target. If your business is growing each year, then chances are your expenses are growing too. Depending on how quickly your expenses are changing, you can update the calculations for your six-month average every month, every quarter, or twice a year. As you build your savings cushion, you can keep the money in your business checking account for easy access or leave a portion of it in a business savings account.

WHEN SHOULD YOU TAKE A BONUS?

Do you know what happens when you increase most people's personal income? They increase their monthly personal expenses. Online business owners are just as susceptible to this trap as anyone else. That is why I have loved seeing how effective bonuses can be for online business owners. Here's why.

If your business is paying you a consistent monthly salary, you will learn how to build your lifestyle around that income just like you would if you were an employee for another company. However, most companies do not pay out juicy bonuses to employees when they perform above expectations. As an online business owner, you can make that a reality.

Bonuses are an awesome way to reward yourself with a larger sum of money when the business is sitting on more cash than it needs. When our clients at Evolved Finance pay themselves a bonus, they are more likely to invest the money, pay off big chunks of personal debt, or build up their personal savings. This is how they make real strides building their personal wealth.

So when should you take a bonus?

When the business is sitting on a savings cushion that goes beyond your three-month savings goal.

For example, if your three-month savings goal is $35,000, and your business checking account has a balance of $50,000, then it would be completely reasonable to give yourself a $15,000 bonus. As long as you save a portion of that $15,000 for taxes, it would not be financially irresponsible to take a bonus of this size on top of your normal salary.

Here are a couple of caveats. If your business has high-interest credit card debt or a loan, you may want to consider paying that down before paying yourself a bonus. Also, if you know that you have some larger onetime expenses coming around the corner, you may want to hold off on taking your bonus until after those expenses have been paid.

With regard to payout frequency, you can do it whenever you want. It is your business after all. However, I recommend reviewing your business's savings cushion every three months to see if a bonus is in order. You could also do biannual or annual bonuses if it makes sense for your business to hold onto the extra cash for longer before distributing a bonus to yourself.

Regardless of how often you take bonuses, there will likely be times where you dip below your three-month savings cushion. This can happen for a number of reasons. Tax bills, large investments in your business, or drops in revenue can all demand that you dip into your savings. This is totally fine. The point of that cushion is for situations just like these. As long as you can build your cushion back up again before you take another bonus, then there is no issue with using your three-month savings to invest back into your business or cover larger expenses.

One last thing to note. It might feel a little weird holding onto this much money in your business. It might even go against advice you have heard from other entrepreneurs. So let's change your mindset around this.

- Yes, you will have to pay taxes on the profit you save up in your business. This is an unavoidable fact of building up your cash reserves. If your tax strategies are such that your business never has any excess cash reserves at the end of the year, you are sacrificing cash flow and financial stability for the sake of saving money on taxes. It is ultimately up to your accountant to guide you around taxes, but you need to be the one to advocate for the financial health of your business if your accountant is only thinking from a tax perspective.

- No, you should not take your three-month savings cushion and invest it in the stock market, crypto, or any other highly volatile investment vehicle. By the time you need the money, your investments could quite easily be worthless. The point of your cushion is that it is liquid, easily available, and not losing value.

- Your three-month savings cushion is an insurance policy. To think that your business will never have a bad month or run into cash flow issues is a form of business hubris. I have seen some very successful online business owners go from being on top of the world to quickly being served a slice of humble pie. You have no idea what the future holds. Plan accordingly.

- Your three-month savings cushion is a testament to your commitment to the long-term health of your business. If your online business is just a quick cash grab, then that is fine. If you want your business to sustain your livelihood for years to come, then your savings cushion is what will enable that to happen.

WHEN SHOULD YOU INCREASE YOUR MONTHLY SALARY?

For most online business owners, simply having a consistent salary and a three-month savings cushion would be an absolutely massive accomplishment. I would agree. If this is not you yet, then this is what you want work toward. That said, there may come a point when taking larger and larger bonuses starts to get a bit silly. Sure, the large chunks of cash are great, but so is knowing that your monthly personal income could be growing as well.

If you are feeling like the time has come to increase your monthly salary, here are the three most common signs that you might be right.

You Are Blowing Past Your Three-Month Savings Goal Each Month

As you should have surmised by now, online businesses can be wildly profitable. They can also grow very quickly. If you set your monthly salary and three-month saving goals, and you are regularly seeing your checking account with far more money than your three-month goal demands, then it might be time to increase your monthly pay.

Your Revenue and Expenses Are Stabilizing

Part of the reason we ask our clients to set reasonable salaries for themselves is because online entrepreneurship can be volatile. Bonuses allow you to reward yourself when you have a really good year while also acknowledging that the growth you had might not be sustainable the following year. In fact, your business might make less money in the following year. However, a good year of revenue and profit might also be a stepping stone toward even better years of revenue and profit in the future. It might mean your business is simply getting better at generating revenue and managing expenses. If it feels like this is the case for your business, then increasing your monthly salary will likely be sustainable.

Your Accountant Tells You to for Tax Purposes

For American readers, paying yourself a monthly salary via payroll is actually part of a tax strategy that can save you thousands of dollars on your tax bill each year (especially as your profits get juicer). Without getting too deep into it, your accountant ultimately has to decide on a "reasonable" salary for you as the business owner to make sure you are following the IRS's rules for this specific tax strategy. If your profits are quickly increasing, then your accountant will likely tell you to increase the portion of your compensation that comes through your payroll salary. If you would like to learn more about this specific tax strategy, talk to your accountant about an "S-corp" tax strategy.

Ultimately, increasing your salary is a side effect of your business generating more profit. Just know that profit can fluctuate, so unless you are ready to decrease your salary down the road, you want to make sure your profit growth is sustainable before reducing your bonuses and increasing your monthly salary instead.

OWNER BENEFITS

In chapter seven, I mentioned a financial concept called owner benefits. I want to share a bit more detail about this concept because it can have an impact on how you look at your total compensation from your online business.

Receiving cash directly from your business, be it through payroll or via profit transfers to your personal bank account, is not the only way your business compensates you. It can also compensate you by paying for business expenses that provide a direct benefit to you personally.

Here are some of the most common owner benefit expenses I see in online businesses. Keep in mind that if you operate a business outside of the United States, some of the expenses may not be valid tax deductions in your country. Also, some of these expenses are deducted in various ways on your tax return depending on how your business is structured.

- Auto lease
- Cell phone
- Computer hardware
- Health insurance
- Home office rent
- Internet
- Owner payroll salary
- Retirement contributions
- Travel
- Utilities (Gas/Water/Electric)

If you have any of the expenses listed above running through your online business, then you are gaining direct benefit by the business paying for these expenses on your behalf. Normally you would be paying for these expenses from your personal income, so the fact your business can potentially use them as tax deductions to lower your tax bill is pretty awesome!

> *NOTE: Please note that your accountant may not be deducting the full amount of these expenses on your tax return even if your business is paying for the full amount of the expense. Also, even if expenses like these are not being paid for through your business, your accountant may still be deducting them at the end of the year.*

If you want to calculate the total compensation you receive from your online business, follow the steps below.

1. Find your total profit number for the year.
2. Find all of the owner benefit expenses in your business for the year and add them all together.
3. Add your total profit and your total owner benefit expenses. The resulting number is the true benefit you are receiving from your business.
4. If you divide the total of your profit and owner benefit by the total revenue your business has generated for the year, you can calculate the percentage of your business's revenue that is benefiting you as the owner.

Here is an example of what the math looks like in practice.

Last year, your business generated $500,000 in revenue. Your profit was $150,000 (a 30% profit margin). Between your cell phone, health insurance, internet, owner payroll, and utilities, your total owner benefit expenses last year were $85,000. Your profit ($150,000) added to your total owner benefit expenses ($85,000) equals $235,000. If you now divide this number by your total revenue of $500,000, you get 0.47. This means 47% of your business's total revenue from last year benefited you as the owner. That is almost half of all the revenue your business generated! Not too shabby!

It is important to keep your owner benefits in mind as you look at your monthly salary and bonuses. If you are not where you want to be yet with your monthly salary or bonuses, you might be gaining more benefit from your business than just your cash compensation.

• ACTION ITEMS •

There is a reason I made this the last chapter of the book. In order to pay yourself responsibly, you have to put into action much of what you have learned in previous chapters. Without visibility into both your personal and business finances, paying yourself a consistent salary that does not also put your business's cash flow at risk is impossible. Let's examine the key action items presented in this chapter so you can take steps toward creating a better plan for your owner's compensation.

- In order to know how much money you need to make to support your lifestyle, you need to gain clarity around your personal financial situation. If you do not have a personal budget yet, go back and read chapter four so you can put together a game plan for how you can better track your personal finances.

- Once you know how much you need your monthly salary to be, you then need to know how much your business can afford to pay you. That is where bookkeeping and financial reporting in your online business become crucial. Chapters five through nine of this book lay out everything you need to know to create a clean financial foundation for your business, to find the right bookkeeper to support you with financial tracking, and to put the Profit Pillars system into your financial reporting system so you can keep your business as profitable as possible. The more profit your business generates, the more it can pay you as the owner.

- To provide yourself with a consistent monthly income, you will need to build up a savings cushion in your business. Per this chapter, I recommend building up enough of a cushion in your business to cover three months of expenses.

- Once you have your three-month savings cushion in your business, you can then consider paying yourself a bonus when the business has more cash than it needs to support your three-month savings. Block off time on your calendar one to four times a year to review your numbers and see if it is time to take a bonus or if it is time to increase your savings cushion due to an increase in your average monthly expenses.

- If you want to see a complete picture of how your business compensates you, reread the last section of this chapter about owner benefits. Carve out some time to review your financials and calculate the total owner benefit you are receiving from your online business.

YOUR SUPPORT SYSTEM

Hot damn—you did it! You read an entire book about the financial side of your online business. Here is what is so awesome about that. Finance does not change. Once you learn and implement the strategies in this book, they will be with you for as long as you are running your online business. Marketing and sales strategies change and evolve as technology and consumer behaviors change and evolve. Finance is different. Finance keeps it old school. Sure, there might be advances in accounting and financial reporting software, but none of that changes the primary financial goal for your online business: make more money than you spend. This is a business principle that will never go out of style regardless of how you generate leads, close sales, or serve your customers.

Do you know what else is awesome? Finance touches every aspect of your business. The more you get comfortable with your numbers, the more you will start to see how every decision you make as an online business owner has an impact on your finances. This will bring a new level of strategy, clarity, and confidence into everything you do in your business. While other online entrepreneurs will admit to finance being their weakness, you have the opportunity to make finance one of your strengths.

If you are serious about making money and building your wealth as an entrepreneur, it sure makes a lot of sense to make finance something you understand and appreciate. That does not mean doing your own taxes or managing your own bookkeeping, but it does mean doing the work that I've presented to you in this book to ensure your financial systems and financial team are an asset to your online business.

Speaking of work, let's talk a bit about implementation.

If you have read this book in its entirety, you now have the full picture of what the four profit pillars framework is all about. However, I hope you come back to reread individual chapters as you implement the different aspects of this book into your financial systems. You cannot execute on all of the action items for all of these chapters at once, so please use this book as a reference guide to find the specific information you need as you need it. For instance, if your business and personal finances are still combined, you will likely want to spend some time rereading chapter six as you clean up that part of your business. Or perhaps reading this book has made you realize that you need to hire a new accountant, in which case you would want to spend your time rereading chapter five.

If you are not sure where to begin with implementation, start with chapter one and skim through each chapter in order. Stop on any chapters where you know you have implementation work to do. Do not move on to the next chapter until you are done. Or you can completely ignore this advice, trust your instincts, and focus on any chapters you think are the biggest priority for your specific situation.

It is also important to remember that you are likely not implementing everything from this book on your own. Whether you need to work on your money mindset, clean up your business's financial foundation, or implement the profit pillars framework into your financial reporting, you will likely need to garner support from one or more of the following people.

YOUR SPOUSE OR LIFE PARTNER

If you share your personal finances with another a person, then any work you do on your personal finances should be discussed with that person. If you need accountability around how you spend (or do not spend) money, then your spouse or life partner could be the best person to help you with that. They might also enjoy spreadsheets and budgeting software more than you, which means they could help you manage your household's personal financial data so that responsibility does not fall solely on your shoulders. Ultimately, as long as you are showing up for the conversation and building a financial plan together, your spouse or life partner has the potential to ease the burden of managing your household finances.

YOUR THERAPIST OR COACH

As we discussed in the first few chapters, so much of our money stories are rooted in childhood and adolescent experiences. Depending on what those experiences were like for you, money might be a deeply triggering and emotional topic. So much so that simply talking with a friend, family member, or partner might not be enough to help you deal with those feelings. That is where working with a therapist or coach to help you reshape your outlook on money can be extremely helpful. Money and entrepreneurship go hand in hand, so if you need more support in dealing with your money mindset, a therapist or coach could be one of your greatest investments.

YOUR BOOKKEEPER

So much of what is covered in this book will mean having a conversation with your bookkeeper about how they organize and present your financial data to you. They are the ones responsible for the data in your bookkeeping software, so they will need to execute on the tactical work of updating your business's bookkeeping processes. You will still need to be ready to communicate any changes in the bookkeeping process you would like to see and potentially even reset some expectations around their services (e.g., getting your reports on time), but you can rest easy knowing that you do not have to be the bookkeeping expert. You just need to communicate the new vision you have for your finances based on what you learned from this book.

If your business is not at the point where you can afford a monthly bookkeeper but you are looking for some guidance around how to make changes to your financial systems based on the principles from this book, there are a number of bookkeepers that offer one-off coaching and consulting services to small business owners just like you.

YOUR ACCOUNTANT

One of the most common reasons business owners of all types get nervous about their finances is because they lack a basic understanding of their responsibilities around taxes. This is where your accountant can help. While their main expertise lies in tax preparation and tax strategy, many accountants also have an advanced understanding of small business finance as well. As I have said many times in this book, if you are worried about the tax implications that might come from implementing strategies from this book, your accountant can support you with any of your concerns.

EVOLVED FINANCE CAN HELP TOO

My team and I at Evolved Finance are also here for support if you need us. There are two ways we can help beyond what you have learned from this book.

1. For any online business owner reading this book, you can purchase our *Profit Pillars* companion course at evolvedfinance.com. It comes with spreadsheets, checklists, and videos that will help you more easily and effectively implement the concepts from this book.

2. For any online business owners operating an online business in the United States, I encourage you to go to evolvedfinance.com and learn about our bookkeeping, tax planning, and tax preparation services. Everything you have learned in this book is the result of the work my business partner, our team, and I have been doing since 2010. Nobody is better equipped to support the financial side of your online business than Evolved Finance.

• • • • • •

I wish I could take you into my brain and show you all of the profit and loss statements I have reviewed and replay all the coaching conversations I have had with online business owners since 2014. I have seen so many online entrepreneurs build profitable and sustainable businesses on the internet that it would change what you think is possible for your own business. It would also change what you think you are capable of learning and understanding as a business owner.

So I hope you believe me when I say you are capable of implementing what you have learned in this book. You are capable of improving the profitability of your business. You are capable of being a more strategic and numbers-oriented business owner without giving up an ounce of your creativity, vision, and passion. In fact, your ability to be creative, expand your vision, and share your passion with the world will only increase as you get more comfortable with your numbers. This has been true not only for the clients we have worked with at Evolved Finance, but for myself and my business partner as well.

With that, I thank you for reading this book. I am so grateful you took a leap of faith and invested your time with me. It is an investment that I hope provides you with a very profitable return.

To your financial success!

ACKNOWLEDGMENTS

I am a big believer that nobody accomplishes anything alone. Without the love, support, and trust of the people below, this book would not exist.

I would like to acknowledge:

My business partner, Corey Whitaker, without whose expertise this book would not be possible. *Profit Pillars* is as much his accomplishment as it is mine. You are the best friend and business partner I could ever ask for.

My wife, Cameron, for supporting and loving me throughout the entire writing process despite my neuroses and anxiety.

My son, Griffin, for keeping me grounded and humble in the way only a toddler can. Dada loves you so much.

My dear friend Anna Whitaker—without your trust and support, this book would not be possible.

My parents, Denny and Gina, for somehow raising me to confidently pursue anything I put my mind to. I could not ask for better parents.

My brother, Brady Stevenson, for being one of the first people to encourage me to quit my job and partner with Corey. Thank you for seeing more in me than I saw in myself at that time.

The Evolved Finance team, who made sure our clients continued to receive world-class service despite my calendar constantly being blocked off for writing sprints. You all never cease to impress and amaze me with your dedication and passion. I am grateful for all of you.

Our current and past clients at Evolved Finance, for trusting our team to manage one of the most vulnerable parts of your businesses.

My friend Nay-nay, for taking such great care of Griff, being a trusted member of my family, and listening to me complain about not getting enough writing done each day.

I would like to also share my gratitude for my book team:

My book proposal coach, Richelle Fredson, for helping me to see the true potential of this book. Your guidance and friendship during the writing process have been invaluable.

My agent, Michele Martin of MDM Management, for taking a chance on a first-time author. Having you in my corner is a gift.

My publishing team at Matt Holt Books (especially my editor Katie Dickman) for believing in my vision to bring financial literacy to online business owners all around the world.

INDEX

A

accountants and accounting firms, 20,
87–89, 95–103, 228. *See also* tax
planning and preparation
accounts payable, 106
ACH transfers, 127
advertising expenses, 43–44, 128,
153–154, 189–191
advertising managers, 154, 156, 190–191
affiliates
expenses, 94, 128, 154, 189, 191
payments to and from, 104, 117, 120,
123, 127–128
amortization expense, 173
attorneys, 99–100, 114, 204. *See also* legal
and professional fees
auto expenses, 55, 66–67, 170, 221

B

bank statements, 82–83, 91
banks and banking, 117, 127–128, 170.
See also checking accounts; savings
accounts
bonuses, 216–219. *See also* distribution of
profit
bookkeepers and bookkeeping
accountant, collaboration with, 93–94
accounting firm services, 87–89
bookkeeper, selecting, 84–90
bookkeeping firms, 89–90
described, 82
freelance, 86–87, 90
importance of, 146
income and expenses, categorizing,
83–84. *See also* Profit Pillars
system

interview questions for hiring, 91–95
need for, 20
online businesses, importance of
familiarity with, 94
Profit Pillars system, transitioning to,
176–177
reconciling accounts, 82–83, 91,
120–122, 155
responsibilities of, 91–92, 227–228
responsiveness, 93
security measures, 92
separation of business and personal
accounts, 50, 111–115
software, 82–83, 85, 91, 93, 106, 121,
178, 207, 228
budgeting for personal finances, 56–57,
59–61, 63–75, 202, 213
business checking account, 50, 56, 62, 80,
112–113, 115–118, 123, 125–127,
200, 216
business entities, 34, 114–115, 130
business owner. *See* owner
business taxes, 173

C

cash flow game (cash flow management),
39–51, 62–63, 124–125, 189
cell phone expenses, 66, 171, 221–222
certified public accountant (CPA), 97–100.
See also accountants and accounting
firms
charitable contributions, 138, 170–171,
173, 175, 202–203
checking accounts
business, 50, 56, 62, 80, 112–113,
115–118, 123, 125–127, 200, 216

checking accounts (*continued*)
PayPal as, 121
personal, 56, 62, 69, 73, 112, 115, 127, 200
checkout software, 50, 78–79, 104–105, 120, 122–124
coaches, teachers, and guest instructor expenses, 128, 159, 162, 193–194
collections, 155
computer expenses, 128, 171, 201, 221. *See also* software
continuing education expenses, 41, 128, 171, 181–182, 203–204
contractors, 83, 95, 104–105, 118, 120, 127–128, 141, 149, 160–164, 166, 171–172, 194–200, 204
cost of goods sold (COGS), 151, 176–177
credit cards
and budgeting, 73
business, 50, 92, 112–116, 118–120, 125–127
customer payments, 120–121. *See also* checkout software; merchant accounts
debt, 6, 15–16, 119, 201–202, 217
fees, 170
financial accounts, 50, 80, 125
interest, 124, 170, 201–202, 217
personal, 50, 73, 115, 202
reconciling financial accounts, 82
separation of business and personal accounts, 50, 112–114
statements, bookkeeper's access to, 92
test transactions, 160
credit score, 119
customer relationship management (CRM), 123

D
DBA (doing business as), 115
debt, 6, 15–16, 81, 119, 125, 197, 201–202, 217
depreciation expense, 173
distribution of profit, 62–63, 80, 216–219
dividends, 62, 80
dues and subscriptions, 171, 173

E
email lists, 145, 187–189
employees. *See also* team expenses
labor costs, 128, 141, 149, 156, 160, 162–165. *See also* labor pillar
meals, 172

payroll expense, 95, 104–106, 128, 164–165, 220–221
as problem-solvers, 204
profitability issues with labor costs, 196–201
taxes, 95
enrolled agent (EA), 97, 99
envelope-based financial system, 116–117
Evolved Finance
budgeting spreadsheet, 72
companion course for *Profit Pillars*, 72, 229
founding of, 3. *See also* Whitaker, Corey
online business expertise, 3, 20, 229
Profit Pillars system for categorizing expenses. *See* Profit Pillars system
services offered by, 19, 33, 85–86, 89, 229
expenses. *See also* specific types of expenses
categorizing, 51, 83–84. *See also* Profit Pillars system
common types of for online businesses, 128
financial visibility, importance of, 32, 34, 46–48, 83–84, 133–134, 146, 223
increase in as revenue increases, 40–42
managing, 126–129
payment methods, 116, 127
as percentage of revenue. *See* percentage of revenue
and profitability. *See* profitability issues
start-up costs for online business, 136–137
and type of business, 129

F
FDIC (Federal Deposit Insurance Corporation), 117
50/30/20 budgeting rule, 64–65
finance
confidence in understanding, gaining, 1–7, 18–22, 49–51
importance of understanding, 3–4, 78–79, 225–226
for online businesses, 17–18, 20, 80–81
financial accounts
checking accounts. *See* checking accounts
checkout software. *See* checkout software

credit cards. *See* credit cards
merchant accounts. *See* merchant
   accounts
opening, 111, 115
reconciling, 82–83, 91, 120–122, 155
simplifying, importance of, 50
types of, 50, 116–126
financial foundation
   action items, 130
   business expenses, managing, 126–129
   components of, 111
   financial accounts, 50, 116–126
   importance of, 53
   separation of business and personal
      finances, 111–115
   simplicity, 3, 5–6, 53, 81, 110–111, 130
financial functions of online business
   action items, 106–107
   bookkeeping, 82–95. *See also*
      bookkeepers and bookkeeping
   finance for online businesses, 17–18,
      20, 80–81
   flow of money, tracking, 80–81
   internal financial operations, 82,
      103–106
   tax planning and preparation, 82,
      95–103. *See also* tax planning and
      preparation
   understanding, importance of, 49–50,
      77–80
financial literacy, 4, 14–20, 22, 46, 79
financial reports
   balance sheets, 92
   bookkeeper's responsibilities, 91–92,
      227–228
   fear of, 33–34
   and financial visibility, 32, 34, 46–48,
      83–84, 133–134, 146, 223
   importance of, 148
   patterns in, 183
   profit and loss statements, 92, 139, 148,
      150–152, 178–179, 183
   purpose of, 33
   reviewing, 206–208
   and use of financial systems, 32–33
financial systems
   author's experience with, 3–6, 133, 193
   envelope-based, 116–117
   and financial reporting, 32–33
   importance of, 48, 77–79
   profit pillars. *See* Profit Pillars system
   simplicity of, 3, 5–6, 53, 81, 110–111,
      130

financial visibility, 32, 34, 46–48, 83–84,
   133–134, 146, 223

G
gifts, 160, 166, 173

H
hardware expenses, 128
health insurance, 66, 221–222
home office, 143, 172, 221

I
income
   categorizing, 83–84. *See also* Profit
      Pillars system
   checking account deposits, 115,
      126–127
   50/30/20 budgeting rule for personal
      expenses, 64–69
   and perceived value as people, 12–13
   percentage of income metrics, 166, 179
   personal sources of, 55–56, 127
   wealth building, 210
independent contractors. *See* contractors
insurance, 66, 128, 170–171, 221–222
internal financial operations, 82, 103–107
internet expense, 66, 221–222
interview questions
   for hiring accountant, 101–103
   for hiring bookkeeper, 91–95

L
labor pillar
   described, 163
   expenses impacting profitability,
      196–201
   independent contractors, 164. *See also*
      contractors
   metrics, 166–169
   as one of profit pillars, 149
   payroll, 95, 104–106, 128, 142–143,
      164–168, 200–201, 213, 220–221
   service-based online businesses, 169
   team morale expenses, 164, 166
launches and promotions, 155, 185, 189, 191
lead and conversion pillar
   common expenses, 153–155. *See also*
      specific expenses
   described, 153
   email list, 187–188
   expenses impacting profitability,
      188–192

lead and conversion pillar (*continued*)
    metrics, 156–158
    as one of profit pillars, 149
lean manufacturing, 109–110
legal and professional fees, 128, 166,
    170–172, 201, 204–205
liability, 113–114, 171
licenses and permits, 173
limited liability companies (LLCs), 114
lines of credit (LOCs), 124–125
live events, 128, 159, 162, 193, 195–196
loans, 124–125, 201–202

M
marketing expenses, 128, 153, 155–156
meal expenses, 128, 172
merchant accounts
    and checkout software, 123. *See also*
        checkout software
    described, 121
    fees, 121–122, 153–155
    as financial account, 50, 125–126
    money transfers between financial
        accounts, 80, 116, 123, 127
    PayPal as, 116, 120–121, 155
    providers, 116, 121, 155
    QuickBooks online invoicing, 116
    reconciling, 82, 120–122, 155
    security measures, 92
    Square, 116
    Stripe, 116, 121, 126, 155
metrics
    labor pillar, 166–169
    lead and conversion pillar, 156–158,
        190
    offer delivery pillar, 160–162
    operations pillar, 173–175
    percentage of income, 166, 179
money, emotional and psychological
    aspects of, 11–14, 24–25, 29, 31–32
money story
    action items, 35
    determining personal money story,
        questions to ask, 30–31
    emotional and psychological aspects of
        money, 11–14, 24–25, 29, 31–35
    factors shaping, 25–30
    and money mindset, 23, 29–30, 34
    personal finances versus business
        finances, 31
    removing emotions from business
        finances, 32–34

O
offer delivery pillar
    common expenses, 158–160. *See also*
        specific expenses
    described, 158–159, 163
    expenses impacting profitability,
        193–196
    and labor expense pillar, 162
    metrics, 160–162
    as one of profit pillars, 149
    service-based business, 162
office furniture expenses, 172
office supply expenses, 128, 172
online entrepreneurs. *See also* owner
    and finance, 1–3, 6, 9, 14–22
    growth, planning for, 197
    money story. *See* money story
    personal finances. *See* personal finances
    risk, 135–136
    separation of business and personal
        finances, need for, 50, 111–115
operations pillar
    common expenses, 169–173. *See also*
        specific expenses
    described, 169
    expenses impacting profitability, 201–206
    metrics, 173–175
    as one of profit pillars, 149
overhead expenses, 136
owner. *See also* online entrepreneurs
    benefits, 142–143, 221–223
    bonuses, 216–219
    distribution of profit, 62–63, 80,
        216–219
    hours worked, 141–142, 197–198
    personal finances, 49, 55–56, 63,
        75, 211, 213–214, 223. *See also*
        personal finances
    salary, 63, 104, 142–143, 164–165, 167,
        200–201, 209–215, 219–220,
        223–224
    taxes, accounting for in determining
        salary and bonuses, 214, 217–218
    total compensation calculation (salary
        plus benefits), 222–223

P
passwords, 92
PayPal, 116, 120–122, 125–127, 155
payroll expenses, 95, 104–106, 128,
    142–143, 164–168, 200–201, 213,
    220–221

percentage of income metrics, 166, 179
percentage of revenue, 152–153, 157–158, 161–162, 167, 174–175, 179, 181–182, 222–223
personal checking account, 56, 62, 69, 73, 112, 115, 127, 200
personal finances
    action items, 74–75
    budget. *See* budgeting for personal finances
    financial goals, 57, 60
    impact of on business finances, 61–63
    income sources for paying personal expenses, 55–56
    and lack of financial literacy, 14–17
    living paycheck to paycheck, 57–59
    and owner's salary, 211, 213–214. *See also* owner
    retirement, 57, 60, 69, 114
    role of in business finances, 49
    saving and investing, 60
    separation of business and personal finances, 50, 111–115
    and spouse or life partner, 55, 71, 73, 214, 227
postage and shipping expenses, 172
pricing, 185–186, 194
printing and fulfillment expenses, 159–160
product development, 159–160, 187, 195
profit
    benefits of running a profitable business, 137–138
    and bookkeeping practices, 147–148
    business problems related to, 181–182
    calculating, 40–42
    and cash flow management. *See* cash flow game (cash flow management)
    distribution, 62–63, 80, 216–219
    in early stages of business, 140–141
    expenses, cutting, 140, 145–146
    growth, investing in, 141
    importance of, 50–51
    and indirect benefits to owner, 142–143, 221–223
    intention and financial visibility, need for, 46–48, 133–134, 146
    pillars. *See* Profit Pillars system
    potential for, 136–138
    profitability issues. *See* profitability issues
    sales, increasing, 144–146

and time put into business by owner, 141–142
    tracking profitability, 138–140, 146
profit and loss statements, 92, 139, 148, 150–152, 178–179, 183
profit margins, 43, 61–63, 136, 138–144, 153, 157, 162, 168–169, 174, 184, 222
Profit Pillars system
    action items, 178–179
    benefits of, 149–150
    bookkeeping, transitioning to Profit Pillars system, 176–177
    companion course at Evolved Finance website, 72, 229
    cost of goods sold (COGS), 151, 176–177
    creation of, 3–4, 193
    described, 6–7, 148–151
    labor expenses, 149, 163–169
    lead and conversion expenses, 149, 153–158
    offer delivery expenses, 149, 158–163
    operations expenses, 149, 169–176
    and profit and loss statements, 92, 139, 148, 150–152, 178–179, 183
    profitability issues, identifying, 183, 207–208
profit-sharing agreements, 195
profitability issues
    action items, 206–208
    identifying, 183, 207–208
    labor expenses, 196–201
    lead and conversion expenses, 188–192
    offer delivery expenses, 193–196
    operations expenses, 201–206
    profitability versus value of business, 134–135
    revenue generation, 184–188
promotions, 155, 185, 189, 191

Q
QuickBooks, 116

R
reconciliation of financial accounts, 82–83, 91, 120–122, 155
rent, 55, 65–66, 128, 142–143, 172–174, 205–206, 221
retirement, 57, 221
revenue
    deposits to business checking and savings accounts, 116–117, 126

revenue (*continued*)
fluctuations in, 210, 218
generating, options for, 185–188
growth, 134, 146, 189–191, 197
percentage of, 152–153, 157–158,
161–162, 167, 174–175, 179,
181–182, 222–223
and profitability issues, 184–188
sources of, 80, 123, 151
revenue game, 38–46
revenue-sharing agreements, 162, 195

S
S corporations, 114, 220
salary expense
action items, 223–224
owner's salary, 209–215, 219–220
owner's total compensation calculation
(salary plus benefits), 222–223
payroll, 95, 104–106, 128, 142–143,
164–165, 167, 200–201, 213,
220–221
payroll expenses, 95, 104–106, 128,
142–143, 164–168, 200–201, 213,
220–221
taxes, accounting for in determining
salary and bonuses, 214, 217–218
and variation in monthly profits,
210–211
sales commissions, 154–156, 189, 192–193
sales reports and sales data, 104–105,
122–124
savings accounts
business, 80, 115, 117–118, 125–126,
212, 215–219
personal, 56, 69–70
security measures, bookkeeping, 92
social marketing, 188
software
bookkeeping, 82–83, 85, 91, 93, 106,
121, 178, 207, 228
budgeting, 64, 71–73, 75, 227
checkout, 50, 78–79, 104–105, 120–124
customer relationship management
(CRM), 123
email marketing, 19, 145
expenses, 128, 145, 152, 171, 173
password management, 92
payroll, 105, 165

personal income tax returns, 95
sales, 104, 122–126
tax preparation, 95
spouse/life partner, 55, 71, 73, 214, 227
spreadsheets
bookkeeping, 84–85, 106, 178–179
budgeting, 57–60, 64, 71–73, 75,
104–105
labor expenses, 166
payroll, 165
in *Profit Pillars* companion course, 72,
229
Square, 116
start-up costs for online business,
136–137
Stripe, 116, 121, 127, 155
supplies expenses, 128, 172

T
tax attorneys, 97, 99–100
tax planning and preparation
accountants, 96. *See also* accountants
and accounting firms
accounting for taxes in determining
salary and bonuses, 214, 217–218
business expenses, 127–128
business taxes, 96, 173
enrolled agents (EA), 97, 99
importance of, 83, 95–97
payroll, 95, 104–105, 220–221
S corporations, 220
savings account for taxes, 118
tax deductions, 78, 94–95, 113, 127,
130, 169–171, 203, 221–222
tax strategy, 41, 81, 89, 96, 99, 101–
102, 104–105, 167, 218, 220, 228
team expenses, 43–45, 160, 166, 168,
196–200. *See also* labor pillar
team morale expenses, 164, 166
therapists, 30–31, 35, 74, 227
travel expenses, 128, 172–173, 205, 221

U
utilities, 128, 143, 172, 221–222

W
website expenses, 128
Whitaker, Corey, 3, 60, 86, 140
wire transfers, 116, 123, 127, 170

ABOUT PARKER STEVENSON

© Joshua C. Mitchell, Your Face Is Red

Parker Stevenson is a co-owner and the CEO of Evolved Finance, a unique accounting firm that offers bookkeeping, tax planning, and tax preparation services for online business owners. Parker lives in San Diego with his wife, Cameron, and his son, Griffin. His journey to becoming an author has been a strange one. After graduating from Loyola Marymount University with a business degree in 2004, Parker chased his dream of being a professional musician while also working for an automotive consulting firm in LA. After his band broke up, he moved back to his home city of San Diego where he began his corporate career at adidas America in their golf division. He would eventually become the Global Commercial Footwear Manager for adidas Golf, only to leave his position in 2014 to help his now business partner, Corey Whitaker, grow Evolved Finance. Due to his years of financial experience in the online space, Parker has coached and advised hundreds of online businesses, including some of the most well-known online entrepreneurs in the industry. He has also done workshops and given talks to thousands of online business owners all across the world.

ABOUT EVOLVED FINANCE

Evolved Finance was founded by Corey Whitaker and his wife, Anna, in 2010. What started as a boutique bookkeeping firm for online business owners has now become the go-to accounting firm for six-, seven-, and eight-figure online business owners all across the United States. After being family friends for many years, Corey would invite Parker into the business in 2014, where Parker would take on his first bookkeeping clients and learn the business from the ground up. Since their partnership, Evolved Finance has gone from a team of four employees based in Southern California to a team of dozens of remote employees located all across the United States. Evolved Finance has reconciled hundreds of millions of dollars in revenue and expenses for hundreds of online businesses and remains the industry leader in accounting services for online business owners in the United States.

If you want to learn more about Evolved Finance's accounting services and/or the companion course for this book, please visit evolved finance.com.

HOW CAN WE HELP?

Evolved Finance is an accounting firm dedicated to helping online entrepreneurs:

- Create financially healthy online businesses through our industry-leading bookkeeping service.
- Maximize their tax savings through our tax planning and preparation services.
- Gain more financial confidence and clarity through our Profit Pillars financial system.

Visit **https://evolvedfinance.com/** to learn about the different ways Evolved Finance can support your online business.

Don't forget to check out the Profit Pillars Course Bundle!

If you want to build a more profitable online business using the framework from this book but **without doing it all from scratch**, then this bundle has you covered! Featuring **powerful spreadsheets, informative video tutorials, and handy cheat sheets**, it's the perfect resource to help you seamlessly integrate the Profit Pillars financial system into your own online business. Visit our website to learn more.